The Best Job-Hunt Book in the World

Max Eggert first read theology at Kings London before transferring his allegiance to Psychology at Birkbeck, from there to Industrial Relations at Westminster and then back to further clinical training in the Department of Psychiatry at Sheffield University.

Having enjoyed a successful career in HR and General Management within Engineering, Construction and Electronics sectors he decided in 1984 to pursue his professional passion in career work assisting consultancies set up in the then new area of support called Outplacement.

Since then Max has assisted many thousands of executives and managers to become successful in their careers through his consultancy Transcareer in the UK and at Interim in Australia where he is Chief Psychologist.

Max has two adult children, lives in Bondi Beach in Australia and Hackney in the UK. His current research interests include clinical hypnosis for personal empowerment, and his other consuming passion is riding his thoroughbred, 'Splinter'. As an Anglican Priest Max is licensed in the Dioceses of Sydney and Chichester as an NSM.

Also by Max Eggert

The Perfect CV
The Perfect Interview
The Perfect Career
Perfect Counselling

RANDOM HOUSE
BUSINESS BOOKS

Max Eggert has asserted his rights under the Copyright, Designs and Patents Act, 1988, to be identified as the author of this work.

The Perfect CV first published in 1992 by Arrow Books
The Perfect Interview first published in 1992 by Arrow Books
The Perfect Career first published in 1994 by Arrow Books

This omnibus edition first published in 2000 by
Random House Business Books,
Random House, 20 Vauxhall Bridge Road, London SW1V 2SA

Random House Australia (Pty) Limited
20 Alfred Street, Milsons Point,
Sydney, New South Wales 2061, Australia

Random House New Zealand Limited
18 Poland Road, Glenfield,
Auckland 10, New Zealand

Random House (Pty) Limited
Endulini, 5a Jubilee Road, Parktown 2193, South Africa

The Random House Group Limited Reg. No. 954009

Papers used by Random House are natural, recyclable products made from wood grown in sustainable forests. The manufacturing processes conform to the environmental regulations of the country of origin.

ISBN 0 7126 8467 0

Companies, institutions and other organizations wishing to make bulk purchases of books published by Random House should contact their local bookstore or Random House direct:
Special Sales Director
Random House, 20 Vauxhall Bridge Road, London SW1V 2SA
Tel 020 7840 8470   Fax 020 7828 6681

www.randomhouse.co.uk
businessbooks@randomhouse.co.uk

Typeset in Poppl-Pontifex by MATS, Southend-on-Sea, Essex
Printed and bound in Great Britain by
Biddles Ltd, Guildford and King's Lynn

For my parents,
Max Heinrich and Elizabeth Owen,
who made possible for me the career
they couldn't have.

Feedback

Theory is all right but it is no substitute for the real thing.

Please write and tell us:

* ★ What you think
* ★ Which CVs you thought were good if you receive them
* ★ What worked for you and what did not if you are a job hunter
* ★ Interview questions which you thought were good
* ★ Any points or tips you would like us to pass on
* ★ What sections need improving

Send your Feedback to:

Max A. Eggert
c/o Random House Business Books
Random House
20 Vauxhall Bridge Road
London
SWIV 2SA

Alternatively, if you would like to visit a careers' doctor, please visit the careers site at www.careerone.com.au

Contents

The Perfect CV

The Best Job-Hunt Book in the World

Contents

The examples – covering letters

The examples – CVs

Chapter 1 The Perfect CV

The Perfect CV is the CV that achieves the interview, no more, no less. When the CV puts your name on the interview shortlist, it has done its job.

We start with a word of warning

Without too much difficulty you can find lots of people only too willing to give you advice on how you should present your career in CV form. In fact, people who give advice on CVs are rather like economists – if you laid us end to end we might go to the moon and back and you would still be given different information. We differ because there are no rules about CVs, no absolutes, only principles and it is these principles which are the subject of this little book.

Some of the suggestions that follow you will love, others

you will abhor. Please be selective because in the end you are going to be the person who will be batting off your CV. It has to be your document and consequently you must feel both comfortable and confident with it.

Make it special

The life of corporate and graduate recruiters is dull enough already without everyone's CV being the same. Make your CV unique and special: take what follows as guidelines rather than ground rules, suggestions rather than shibboleths.

There is no bible or Ten Commandments on how to write CVs, but only ideas and concepts which have been proven in the job market by thousands of job hunters with whom I have been privileged to work.

You will receive as many different pieces of advice on your CV as the number of people to whom you show it. Before you take the advice ask yourself the Quality Control Question:

When did the person giving this advice last gain a job for themselves or for someone else on the basis of what they are telling me to do?

If their job success or experience is not recent, handle the information you are given with care.

Chapter 2 The CV is the Ticket to the Job Race

The CV is not only the first thing the potential employer sees about you; more significantly it is the only part of the whole job selection process over which you as a job seeker have 100 per cent control. You can't control the availability of the sort of job you want, you can't control who gets shortlisted, you can't control the interview – although you might if you read another book from this series, *The Perfect Interview*. No, you can only control how you look in your CV.

The ticket to the job race

Your CV won't win you the job because it is rare for anyone to get hired just on the strength of their CV alone, but your CV will get you the ticket to the job race. Your CV is the ticket to the candidacy, so it goes without saying that it should be letter perfect, neat, easy to read and well organized. Even if you achieved just that, your CV would be, in my experience, better than 60 per cent of those which are sent by job hunters today.

Chapter 3 Looking To Turn You Down

Remember from the outset that at the CV stage of selection the recruiter is looking for reasons to turn you down and not to take you on! Advertisements these days are going to attract hundreds of applications, sometimes thousands of replies is not that uncommon.

As a recruiter, if I have a pile of CVs, my main task is to reduce the mountain of 'job hopefuls' to a molehill of 'job possibles'. So that the maxim 'when in doubt, throw it out' is very much used by recruiters.

See me, see me!

The recruiter always thinks that he or she is good at their job simply because it never emerges how good the person, whose CV has just been rejected, might have been. Recruiters never gain any negative information about potentially brilliant candidates they have passed over at the sort stage. So right from the very start your CV has to be special, and state in as many ways as possible 'see me, see me.'

Chapter 4 No Gain Without Pain

'I got so fed up with writing my CV and then keeping it up to date' is a frequent cry of the job hunter. It is amazing that some people want to get a lifetime's career into a CV that takes less than one hour to write.

If you get bored with writing your CV just think how boring it is to read CVs day after day.

Eighteen million CVs

Here is a simple sum:

$$\frac{20\% \text{ of } 1.5 \text{ million} \times 5}{1,000 \times 2} = 750$$

Let me explain why you should have this number in mind when

you are writing your CV. Say there were 1.5 million people unemployed and looking for work. Say that just one in five bother to write a CV. And supposing they send off just five CVs a week for 12 weeks, that is one per day for the average time it takes to gain a job. That is a staggering 18 million CVs in any one three-month period. If only half of those are sent to blue-chip firms in *The Times* Top 1000 firms, then that means that those firms are being sent something like 750 CVs a week. Now reading 750 CVs each week is what I call really boring. For your CV to have any chance of success, it has to be something very special.

Your CV has to be like a young plant in a tropical forest reaching up to the light. If it is to survive, it must use every tip and strategy that it can. In addition it must be realized that although there are no short cuts to the CV, the investment in time and effort will be well rewarded.

Chapter 5 How many CVs?

In an ideal world there should be one CV specifically written and customized for each job, but today's job market requires you to send off hundreds of CVs to potential employers because competition is fierce and quality opportunities are scarce. Consequently, the CV has to be somewhat ubiquitous.

In my experience the serious job hunter needs 3 basic CVs, namely:

1   A CV built around your present job
2   A CV aimed at the next job in your career
3   A combination of 1) and 2) above

Keeping track

Make sure you remember which CV you have sent to which employer. It sounds easy enough, but an amazing number of applicants forget. Some careful administration is needed here.

Chapter 6 The Words

Curriculum Vitae
From the Latin, which is 'The way your life has run'.

Résumé
From the French, meaning 'summary'.

For the job seeker a CV is a personal document outlining pertinent information needed by a prospective employer. It is to enable the employer to tell quickly whether or not a meeting would be worthwhile. If what is seen is liked, it will lead to an interview. If not, it won't and you and the selector will have both been saved the time and effort of an interview.

Basic requirements

As with most of life, there are no absolutes and CVs are no exception. There are things which work in the job market and things which do not. What follows are some practical tips and ideas which have justified their inclusion throughout trial and error in the job market. The CV serves three basic requirements:

★ To highlight your value to a potential employer
★ To provide a structure and a curriculum for the interview
★ To act as a record of the substance of the interview

Writing a CV is not difficult but if it is to achieve its purpose it will require time, effort, reflection, creativity and determination.

Above all, the CV must be written with the potential employer firmly in mind. Authors write with their readers in mind, advertisers with their potential customers in mind, and so must you. You are selling your skills and experience in the job market, and you must ensure that your personal brochure presents you in the best possible way to your potential buyer.

Chapter 7 Corect Speling

I bet the heading on this page jarred! It is obvious that everything in the CV has to be spelt correctly but you would be surprised how many have mistakes in them.

When you are only represented by two or three pages of A4 it takes just one small error for the selector to put you in the 'Polite Turn Down' pile.

What spelling mistakes say about you

All sorts of things are incorrectly inferred from a spelling or typing mistake, including:

* ★ You cannot spell
* ★ You are lazy
* ★ You are inattentive to detail
* ★ You want to fail
* ★ You could not represent the company
* ★ You do not really want the job

There will be enough reasons for the recruiter to put you in the 'No' pile without you providing by misspelling or the odd 'typo' an additional reason.

It is not enough to run the CV through the spell check. This will catch the spelling errors but not the 'typos' and a typo will have the same effect on a selector as a spelling error.

SEW KNOW MOOR ARROWS!

Chapter 8 Short Sentences

Make your CV easy to read. That means short sentences. Long sentences are complicated. Long sentences are difficult to read. Short sentences can be skimmed quickly.

Unless you are going for a job as a writer, facts are more important than style. The tabloid press approach is the best. Short sentences have power. The active tense is best. Remember you only have 60 seconds to get your message across. Do not make the reader work. Make your CV easy to read. Use short sentences.

Chapter 9 Positive and Minus

With a little bit of thought, it can be recognized that certain words are far more positive in their impact than others of roughly the same meaning.

For example:

negotiated is stronger than liaised
managed is more positive than supervised
controlled is better than responsible for

Once the CV has been written every word needs to be examined carefully to see whether another more powerful or positive equivalent can be used.

A passive attitude

Generally speaking, the weaker words occur when the job holder is either passive or reactive to the work situation rather than in control of things.

Here are some more examples:

maintained	prevented	rejected
ordered	provided	revamped
performed	recommended	specified
prepared	rectified	supported

There is nothing intrinsically wrong with these words, but they give the impression of a passive person, someone who responds to situations rather than initiating them. With a little more thought and research more positive synonyms can be found and used to create a completely different impression – it is not what you do but the way you present it!

Chapter 10 You Have the Right to Remain Silent

Remember, you do not have to tell the selector everything. One of the reasons that CVs fail is because they are far too long. Why is it that police forces around the world say 'You have the right to remain silent'? Because the more you say, the more you will entrap yourself. In CV terms the more you write, the more reason you give the selector to turn you down.

So keep it brief. How brief is brief? – well, as a rule of thumb, if you say it all in two or three pages at the most there must be something wrong. There are many advisers who would say that just one page is all it takes. My view is that the more senior you are, the shorter your CV can be. Richard Whittington, for example, could get away with just the line 'Thrice Lord Mayor of London' and get a job as a City banker.

Our consultancy record to date is a 17-page CV which we had presented to us in Edinburgh. Not only was it 17 pages long, it was not until you waded through to page 16 that you discovered what it was exactly that the writer was currently doing.

The 'must see' decision

The CV is a personal brochure and not your autobiography. How many product brochures tell you all the bad points as well as the good? Same with CVs; you need to give the selector only enough information to make the 'must see' decision. No more, no less.

There are no absolutes, but a reasonable rule of thumb is minimum of one page if you are a senior executive, two pages if not, and for everyone four pages maximum including a technical page if you are in engineering, computing or similar.

The CV is often used to provide a structure to the job interview. This purpose is frequently ignored or unappreciated by the job seeker. If you tell an employer you failed one of your A levels then the employer will talk about your failure. It is in your best interests to include only positive information and not feed the interviewer with negative points.

So you have a good deal of freedom to leave out information. What do you drop? Well, first of all, anything that is negative. Negative information is best explained at the interview when you have at least a fighting chance of explaining yourself.

If, for instance, you were fired five years ago because you disagreed with your boss but have had a fantastic career since, there is no rule that says you have to declare your dismissal on your CV. If you get asked at the interview why you left the firm five years previously you can then explain the circumstances.

The 'golden decade'

Let me give an example. We live in a period which unfortunately and unwisely discriminates on age. Now if you think that your age is the most important thing which will commend you to an employer, then by all means put your date of birth immediately after your name and address.

This will go a little hard on you though if you live on the other side of what is called the 'golden decade' which is 30–40 for men, and because this world is sexist as well as ageist, 25–35 for women, then your chances of getting on the shortlist are somewhat slim.

Put information about your age on the back page. I would suggest you consider doing this anyway since there are few jobs in which how old you are is more significant than your academic qualifications or what you do. A word of caution – do not *omit* essential information such as age. Employers have a way of reading the wrong information into omissions – no age stated therefore he must be an oldie!!

People in the computer industry have a good phrase, 'user friendly', and that is what your CV should be – user friendly, easy to work with. For example, if you have a higher qualification then please don't tell me that you first went to Monks Orchard Primary School and then on to Norbury Manor to get your GCSEs. Make yourself easy to work with by starting with your highest qualification first and going backwards. If you have a degree I know that you must have 5 GCSEs and 2 A levels or the equivalent.

What often happens is that on leaving college many people prepare a CV for the first time. From then on, when the person wishes to change jobs their current employment information is tacked on to the college CV and it grows and grows like Topsy.

Each time you make a trip into today's highly competitive job market, make a fresh start on your CV.

The reverse chronology rule

Let us get back to being user friendly. Ask yourself the question:

> *'Which is more relevant to a prospective employer of my choice – what I did when I left school or what I am doing now?'*

or

> *'Where are the skills and abilities I am currently selling – in my current job or in the one I took when I left school?'*

The most recent experience is for most people the most relevant to their job hunt. So use this by employing the reverse chronological rule when writing about career and achievements. Whilst talking about career, doesn't that sound better than 'experience or work', and even better doesn't the heading *Career and Achievements to date* imply something strong in that it is saying,

> *'This is what I've done so far but I still have much to give.'*

Everybody has 'experience' but it sounds uninteresting on a CV. Achievements are far more powerful. We shall be returning to achievements later in the book but I want now to return to some suggestions about the layout of the career section of the CV.

The Best Job-Hunt Book in the World

Chapter 11 Layout: Framed

Sometimes CVs give the impression that they have been shoe-horned on to the page. The content could be excellent but the visual presentation is awful. In the better restaurants food is arranged on the plate to look as good as it tastes. Food for interviewers ought to be arranged using the same principles – to make it look attractive.

If you look at a picture which has been framed, the margin at the bottom of the picture is usually larger than at the top or the sides. Look at the two diagrams in Figure 1:

The one on the right is much more visually attractive. Lay out your CV in the same way.

Getting the right layout

Back pages of CVs are frequently only partially filled. This is a waste of opportunity to be able either to add relevant information or to spread your information so that it appears more attractive.

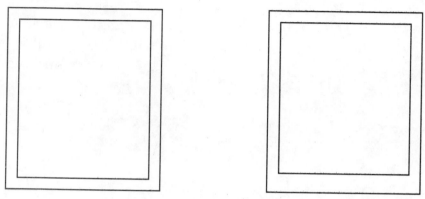

Figure 1

Half close your eyes and look at your CV – does the block of information look lopsided? Play about with the layout so that you gain a centrally balanced picture. See the diagrams below:

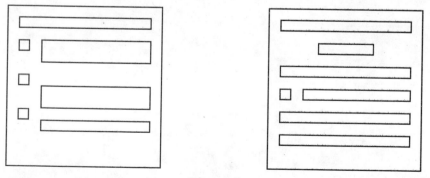

Figure 2

Again, it is the CV on the right which will create a better impression.

Everything counts

Now, I know that it is nonsense to suggest that decisions by recruiters are made on visual impression and not on content. Of course, the content is by far the most important, but everything counts. If I have the job of sorting through six or seven hundred CVs and after I have been working for an hour or so I come across a messy CV which is poorly laid out, the temptation to move on to the next CV is often too great. Why should the selector spend time on your CV when the next one in the pile looks much more attractive?

Having worked hard on the content, make sure you present it in the most visually attractive way.

Chapter 12 To Justify, Or Not To Justify

Unless you want to show off your WP or DTP skills I would suggest that you do not right hand justify your CV. There are several reasons for this.

First, if your CV is justified, it looks as if it is one of hundreds that you have produced. We know it is, but let the prospective employer think that your CV has been specially created and is a one-off.

An outsider trying to get in

Second, working documents in industry and commerce are not usually right-hand justified so when your CV arrives with its clean-cut right-hand margin, you are saying in a quiet way that you are an outsider trying to get in.

Finally, the ragged right-hand edge looks more visually

interesting than the boxed edge made by a right justification.

The best thing to do is to make sure that the CV looks good. Try two versions, justified and unjustified, and go with the one that looks the better.

The Best Job-Hunt Book in the World

Chapter 13 Quality Paper

Would you turn up to the interview in your gardening clothes? Of course not, but it is surprising how many people submit CVs on cheap photocopying paper, usually 'borrowed' from their current employer.

Not that you are going to secure the interview on the basis of the quality of the CV paper, but image and first impression are increasingly important these days.

Plain white A4

Your CV should be on white standard A4 paper because that is what almost every organization uses today. For a PR or marketing job, perhaps a pastel or stronger colour could be used, but it is safer with plain white A4 of the best quality you can afford.

Do you really wish to have your personal brochure on cheap paper? No, you don't. Your CV paper should match your interview clothing in that it should be the best you can afford and that goes for the paper for the covering letters and the envelopes as well.

The Best Job-Hunt Book in the World

Chapter 14 Don't No. 1 – References

Don't include a reference

Job seekers often feel obliged to include references in their CV but it is obvious that any referee provided by the job hunter is bound to be friendly. Thus there is little advantage to the employer writing to a referee who has been nominated by the applicant. I have not come across an applicant yet who has invited a prospective employer to write to someone who will not provide a positive comment about the job seeker's work, attitude and disposition.

Employers are mainly interested in the relevance of your skills, experience and, more importantly, your atitudes, commitment and motivation. So while a member of the aristocracy may be impressive, or a local MP, police commissioner or other dignitary, they are not likely to be able to speak directly as to your suitability unless, of course, you want to go into politics or the police.

Consequently, if you feel bound to mention references then the simple statement, 'References available on request' should suffice.

Minimal information

Following a decision in the House of Lords against an employer who gave a true, but damaging, reference to another employer about a potential employee, most employers, or their personnel departments, will only give minimal information. Employers are usually more interested in qualitative data than quantitative. How hard you worked, or what aspect of your work you found interesting or did well is far more telling than bald statements of your job title and how long you spent in that job.

For these reasons, most references are taken up over the telephone and given off the record. In spite of the fact that most large firms have policies about not providing references except through the personnel department these rules are not always kept.

What would one of your previous bosses say about you if he or she was asked:

★ What did he actually do?
★ How well did he do it?
★ What was her major contribution to the department?
★ How did she get on with other people?
★ Was he a self starter?
★ Could she be left unsupervised?

Obviously the truth will out but you can certainly help the truth along in a variety of ways.

Your ideal reference

After you have completed your CV a useful discipline is to write out your ideal reference for yourself. What would you like your previous boss to say about you? How could you justify all the points you wanted made about your work and your approach to it? Once you have done this, I would suggest you telephone your potential referees and bring them up to date with your career aspirations, plans and actions. (This is not always appropriate with present employers except in some public sector jobs where you are expected to move on regularly). Having told your referees about your plans you can then refresh their memory about your recollections of your performance, with statements like 'You remember when I did "x", you said it was good because . . .' will at least help them recall your good points. After you have spoken to them ensure that they have a copy of your CV as a reminder of all your achievements.

Particularly important when you want to change your career is to emphasize those aspects of your job and skills profile which are allied to your new sphere of aspirations.

Chapter 15 Don't No. 2 – Photographs

What you must remember here is that for most of our history as humans we have been swinging around in trees, painting wode on ourselves and eating each other. Our primal instincts have taught us to look at another person and very quickly form an opinion about that person. We think yes – no, good – bad, like – dislike. In certain states of the US, employers are legally forbidden to ask candidates to send a photograph, simply because opinions form very quickly on visual information alone. So unless you were blessed by birth by being in the top five per cent for traditional good looks and are photogenic, you're likely to fall victim to visual discrimination. If the research finds that traditionally good-looking criminals get shorter sentences than ordinary-looking criminals, then what chance have you got as an applicant if, like the rest of us, you are just average in the looks department?

The media is an industry committed to stereotype and

image making. Every newscaster is both handsome and authoritative. Someone could be an eight stone weakling and still be able to read the news, but I've not seen one yet. If you are just ordinary to look at, and most of us are, do not include a photograph.

A professional, not a booth

If a photograph is called for then invest money on this aspect of the job search project. The photographic booths in railway stations do a great job in producing snaps for passports and travel cards but they are not good enough for CVs. Go to a professional portrait photographer and tell him or her exactly what you want. Take along pictures from business journals or company corporate literature that you like and brief the photographer on the image you wish to project. Sometimes it is helpful to decide on three adjectives to describe the image you feel you have or you wish to project and tell the photographer that you want to look

competent, dynamic and hardworking

or

professional, thorough and reliable

or

creative, enthusiastic, dynamic

Whatever three words suit you, and are appropriate to the type of job you are pursuing, ask to be photographed in a half smile. People looking at photographs of individuals with a half smile rate them as more intelligent, more friendly and with better interpersonal skills. The sort of things you would want in an employee anyway.

Have glasses, look intelligent

Secondly, if you normally wear glasses, wear them for the photograph because again you get rated as more intelligent than those who don't wear them.

Experts tell us that we should wear darker clothes to look more powerful. The point here, of course, is that you should think carefully about what you wear and the image or expectations it will create.

However, the basic rule still is: don't include a photograph unless you have to and if you must send a photograph spend money on getting it right.

Chapter 16 Don't No. 3 – Salary

The iron rule of wages says that employers will pay you as little as they can to get you, motivate you and prevent you from leaving. Salary, then, is a negotiation point and to get this in perspective we must take a small excursion into the rules of negotiation (because I presume you wish to gain as much as salary as you can for your services).

The second rule of negotiation is 'only negotiate from power' (the first being only negotiate with decision-makers). When you are one of 150 or so other candidates who respond to a job advert, you have no power. So then is not the time to mention salary or what you want.

When you get on the shortlist you are one of perhaps five people but this is still not the time to mention pay and conditions.

Now, supposing you are the last candidate in the ring, do you have power? You bet. If the prospective employer turns you down now he or she knows that the whole recruitment process is going to start all over again and that is worth real money to you.

As late as possible

Always, always, always leave salary negotiation as late as possible in the selection process. The little 'c' before the salary section in an advert for a job stands for 'circa' and in salary terms that can mean as much as ten per cent above or ten per cent below. Remember – if you start on a low salary with a firm you will stay low. One of the reasons for changing jobs is to improve your financial situation so employers expect you to negotiate. This point is covered in great detail in *The Perfect Interview*, but for the time being don't include a figure for expected salary on your CV.

You may be writing to one of those firms that gives a low basic wage but lots of benefits – like a super fully serviced car, mortgage subsidy, your telephone bill paid and holidays which can be linked to business trips to the company's offices in the West Indies, Miami or Hong Kong. They are offering a basic £20,000 plus all these add-ons. They see from your CV that you are earning £22,000 without all the benefits but do not shortlist you because you are earning too much! So please, don't include salary. If you insist on putting something then I would suggest the phrase 'Salary is negotiable at interview'.

What the professionals require

Sending your CV to agencies and headhunters, however, is different. These firms are paid a commission (sometimes as high as 35 per cent) of first year's earnings. They have a vested interest in getting as much for your 'head' as possible. In the salary stakes they are going to be on your side, so provide them with details of current package and, of course, what you would like to earn. You will get the benefit of some realistic feedback on your market worth.

Letting agencies know how much you earn and how much you expect (or will move for) does not preclude salary negotiations with your employer.

Chapter 17 Be Unique

If the employer writes the advert well and specifies exactly what is required then about 80 per cent of the CVs that are received will be from people like yourself who actually fit the specification. You will have had the same qualifications, the same sort of experience, so how can you appear different in a positive way? I would suggest from your achievements in a non-work situation – particularly if you have held an office or a position to which you were elected. For example:

Elected Treasurer of the College Geological Society
Elected Secretary of the PTA
Elected to the Committee of XYZ

What does this term 'elected' mean? It says in a very quiet way – 'Look, my peers and colleagues outside the work context think that I am reliable, honest, responsible and trustworthy enough to be elected and to serve them in this or that capacity.'

Sporting achievements

Now, not all of us hold public offices or are members of the Rotary Club, the Lions or Mothers Union – although, if you are, they are worth mentioning. What about sporting achievements current or past? Even if you are past 50 years you can always tuck in somewhere that you represented your house, school or team at some particular sport.

I have worked on the CV of a Scotsman and a South African. The first acted as coach for the volleyball national team and the second was captain of a national youth team. Neither had his considerable sporting achievement on his CV.

What about your interests? You could put 'reading', but how much more interesting if you put

The English Novel prior to 1930

or

Modern autobiographies post 1952.

The football club administrator

I recently met a lady who had a very modest job in a lighting factory in Wiltshire. Twenty years previously, because her son was fanatical about football and had no one to play with, she organized first a football team, then a league and is now administrator of the town's local football club which is affiliated to the Football Association. Now, if I were an employer looking for good administration skills, interpersonal skills and determination, her achievements outside work would say it all.

Chapter 18 More Interest in Interests

Just two more things on outside interests and activities. (Not too many, otherwise the employer might think that you will not have time for work.) What you spend your disposable income on or your free time on tells a potential employer a great deal about you, your values, your motivation and, in some cases, your intelligence.

For instance, suppose someone had as her interests

★   Bridge at county level
★   Crosswords
★   Software design

she is likely to be

★   Intellectually able
★   Good at problem solving
★   Precise and possibly competitive

Suppose someone had

★ Squash
★ Entertaining
★ Restoring classic cars

he is likely to be

★ Competitive
★ Sociable
★ Possibly practical

Let colleagues have a say

What interests will you declare on your CV? Ask some friends at work – who do not know you socially – 'What image does this create for you of someone?' and then give them your three interests. Is what they say the image you want to present?

Don't forget, the primacy rule works here as well. Here is an example:

★ Translating medieval German mystery plays into English
★ Television – especially drama
★ Family – enjoying my young children

gives a completely different picture to the following:

★ Family
★ Television
★ German translations

The last point on interests really applies to the whole CV. Remember interviewers eat what you feed them. If it is in your CV then be prepared not just to be asked questions about what you have written but to be tested to destruction.

Be prepared – to expand

Woe betide you if you can't expand in detail on what you put down. Frequently, when I was a full-time recruiter, I would see that someone had put reading as an interest and then at interview was unable to tell me quickly what was the last book they read. I once asked a young man at Sussex University to tell me about his interest in films, only to be told that he had seen a certain Clint Eastwood film all of three times. If you fail the credibility test in one part of your CV, it contaminates the whole CV. Just like those people at interview who use the phrase, 'Well, to be really honest . . .' and make you wonder about the veracity of the whole interview. Be prepared to talk fluently in the interview about your interests.

Chapter 19 The Whole Truth

As I've said before, interviewers eat what you feed them and as most interviewers are not trained in this basic management skill, you can expect your CV to form the basic structure of the interview. It is absolutely paramount that everything on your CV can be verified and is true. If you cannot justify or speak to any part of your CV, your entire credibility will be lost and your chances of a job offer will be minimal.

No fiction, please

Omissions are permissible. That is to say, you can leave out negative information but be prepared to be challenged on the 'gaps' during the interview.

Just as you would not wish to join an employer who lied about your salary or career prospects, by the same token you should not invent qualifications you do not have or fictitious employment. These things are easily checked and, even if you are taken on, could be used as grounds for dismissal.

The Best Job-Hunt Book in the World

Chapter 20 Use the Back Page and Put it on the Right

If you must say something which is not in your favour, then here are two tips. First put the bad news on the back page; and second, put it on the right-hand side.

Putting it in perspective

Put it on the back page so that at least the selector will read all the good stuff first, and any potentially negative information can be put into its appropriate perspective. For example, if the positions which you are applying for usually require someone of graduate status, and you have no degree but you have the appropriate experience, then structure your CV so that your career outline and details appears before the section on your education.

Now let me explain why the right-hand side of your CV

should be used. CVs are usually skimmed not read. They are gone through very quickly to gain a shortlist pile and a somewhat larger PTD (Polite Turn Down) file. When people skim for information, because they read from left to right, the left-hand side of the CV is read with far more attention and accuracy than information appearing on the right-hand side.

Chapter 21 Career Summary

Constructing the career summary is perhaps the most important and significant preparation for the CV. Whether or not you decide to use a career summary in your final CV, it is still a very useful discipline.

A career summary is a simple statement of twenty or so words that encapsulates your career aspirations and what you wish to sell in the market place. Imagine that you only have thirty or so words to convince a prospective employer to listen to what you have to say. This process will concentrate the mind and focus the reader on what exactly it is you wish your CV to project.

The summary brings three potential benefits:

★   First, it will help you become quite clear on which of your skills you wish to utilize and the shape of the career or job you want.

- ★ Second, when placed strategically after your name, address and telephone number, it will act like a banner headline for your CV. In jargon terms, it acts as a pre-conditioning statement, that is, it conditions the reader to anticipate positive information about you.
- ★ Third, a career statement can be used rather like a go/no-go gauge in quality control. Everything that you wish to put on your CV should in some way support and justify the career statement. If you wish to include something about yourself which does not match the criteria of your career summary, then it may be wise to censor the item.

Developing a thirty-word career statement starting with a blank page can be quite a difficult exercise so you might like to try the following approach using a 'mind map' and the 'mnemonic' for the SAKE of your career.

SAKE

SAKE stands for the four different areas of yourself in which a prospective employer has an interest, namely your:

- ★ Skills
- ★ Attitudes
- ★ Knowledge
- ★ Experience

So here is the procedure:

1 Take a sheet of A4 paper and put your name in a circle in the centre and then from the circle four arms coming off

with Skills, Attitudes, Knowledge and Experience (see figure 3).

2   Now, just think about yourself in these areas, in terms of what you have, what you have done and what you have to offer a future employer. Let your imagination ebb and flow, jotting down anything and everything that comes to mind.

You can show your mind map to your partner, to a good friend or a business colleague whose views you value, because we sometimes miss the obvious or even devalue what we have to offer.

3   Next, go through your mind map, first taking out all the things you don't want to do, or use. Having done this, then rank in order all those aspects about yourself a potential employer would be interested in. This will give you the curriculum for your career summary.

4   Write your career summary in the third person singular as if you were an employment agency sending out details about yourself to a potential employer. (See page 59 and Chapter 49).

5   Continually revise your career statement until you feel comfortable with it.

Figure 3 Personal Career Statement

Develop a mind map for your career to date, using the structure below

On Figure 4, you will see an example of how this structure has been used by a computing specialist.

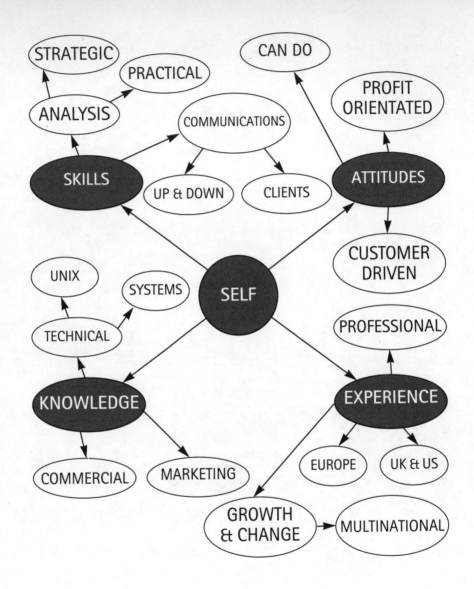

Figure 4 Personal Statement Mind Map

By playing with these concepts this individual was able to develop the career statement below.

Career summary

A senior marketing professional with significant management experience gained with major US and European high technology multinationals.

An effective thinker and doer offering proven strategic planning, business management and communication skills. Able to work effectively at all levels in organizations with the ability to manage change and achieve commercial profit targets.

Further examples of career statements can be found in Chapter 49.

Chapter 22 First Things First – Again

If you were a prospective employer what would be significant if you were looking for an employee? Put these facts in order of importance:

★ Who you worked for
★ When you worked for them
★ What you actually did

I'm sure you came up with the right answer, which is:

★ What you did
★ Who you did it with
★ When you did it

And yet we rarely see the individual's career history set out in this way in CVs.

Setting it out

It makes sense to put on the left-hand side what you did – recalling what I said about reading from left to right, put the important things on the left. In the centre of the page goes the organization that you work for – you don't need the address at this stage, it takes up too much room – and the dates go on the right-hand side. If you have had lots of jobs and you are worried about seeming to be a job hopper, or if you are a woman returner who has had a career break, you are more likely to create a favourable impression this way.

Career titles

You remember what I said about the eye skimming? Well, not only does it skim from left to right, but also from top to bottom. If on the left-hand side you just have a list of dates this does not convey very much information, but if I can see a list of career titles this creates an impression. In the following two examples, for instance, if I just skip down the left-hand side of the page and see:

1   Regional Sales Director
     Sales Manager
     Sales Rep
     Sales Administrator

2   D.P. Manager
     Operations Manager
     Senior Analyst
     Analyst/Programmer
     Programmer

At a glance a whole career unfolds, presenting the impression of a career which is still advancing and not of someone who only stays in a job a short while before moving on.

The Best Job-Hunt Book in the World

Chapter 23

Achievements, Not Just Responsibilities

People are sometimes too lazy to write their own CVs, and just crib one from their job descriptions by writing down all their responsibilities. I suppose that is better than nothing, but anybody can be given responsibilities. It does not really say what you did or did not do. You should also remember that when personnel departments write job descriptions they are doing so for use in pay grading and appraisal assessment, not so that an individual can get a job elsewhere. Who in their right mind would want a CV that includes information written by someone else? It is rather like trying to sell a product using the raw material procurement specification and not developing any sales literature.

When you write about your job don't say what someone else asked you to do based upon your job description but say what you actually did and how good you were at it.

The achievement principle

This we call the achievement principle. A storeman may be responsible only for stock, but a reduction in slow moving stock of 17 per cent and inventory levels reduced by 50 per cent are achievements.

Taking charge of sales in Surrey and Kent is a responsibility; continually selling over target by not less than 15 per cent in any one period is an achievement.

Basically, what you are claiming by highlighting an achievement is 'Look, I did this for them, I can do it again for you.' Lord Byron said something along the lines of 'If you want to know what a man will do in the future, look to his past'. In psychology we say the best predictor of future performance is past performance. So what we are saying here is – make your CV achievement rich.

Chapter 24 Achievements are FAB

There is a very simple process for getting your achievements down. It is called FAB – F stands for 'Feature'; A for 'Analysis'; and B for 'Benefit'.

F for 'feature'

First of all, list all the things that you have actually done in a job. All those special successes, the times when you thought to yourself, 'I really did well there' or 'I really earned my salary there'. These are the highlights of your job. These are all the 'F's for Feature.

Add in the numbers

Now, we must work on the A. A is for 'Analysis'. We must analyse the feature. What was it, how big was it, who was involved, what were the savings to the company? Ask yourself the question, 'Is there any way I can get a number attached to the feature – a quantity, a percentage, anything that can be measured?' Reasons for this are both simple and obvious. If an achievement has a number attached to it, it looks more impressive, more credible and more understandable. For instance, we could take the achievement:

Supervised the research of microbiologists

Let's work with that. How many microbiologists, what grade were they, what type of research, how did you supervise them? Working through this type of question we get to this achievement:

*Supervised a multi-disciplinary team of eight
graduate microbiologists, directing research into
enzyme technology.*

Help the gatekeepers to say 'yes'

As a personnel manager in charge of recruitment, I might not know much about microbiology or enzyme technology, but I do understand the words multi-disciplinary and directing and the number eight. So not only does it sound more impressive, you help those people we call 'gatekeepers' to say 'yes'. Gatekeepers are people like those in personnel or human resources who control the gate through which candidates pass into the firm.

They don't have the final say in who gets taken on but they do have a power to say who gets seen.

So a quick recap: which sounds better to you?

Supervised the research of microbiologists

or

Supervised a multi-disciplinary team of eight graduate microbiologists directing research into enzyme technology.

I know which I would prefer.

Selling the sizzle

Let's now deal with the B. This comes straight from an established sales technique which suggests that people don't buy features, but do buy benefits.

For instance, I don't buy my car because it is a Turbo version, has a sun roof and central locking, I buy it because:

I can accelerate quickly, have fresh air in the car on a hot day and when I park I can secure the car easily.

In other words, I want the benefits brought by the features, not the features themselves – so sell the sizzle not the sausage.

So – what?

It does not always work, but in the achievements section you should try to get in as many benefits to the company as possible. Use a very simple mechanism to do this. Ask yourself the question 'So what?' – 'So what was the company able to do that it could not do before?' 'So what was the advantage gained by the company as a result of this achievement?' Perhaps an example will help me explain. The basic achievement is:

Raised venture capital.

Add the 'A' for Analysis:

Raised £5m venture capital from Holland and the City.

Add 'B' for Benefit:

Raised £5m venture capital from Holland and the City, enabling the company to grow without the requirement to consolidate the European expenses on the US balance sheet.

The Personnel Manager doing the initial selection might not know too much about balance sheet consolidations, but it sounds good, doesn't it?

An engineering example

Let's take an engineering example:

Here is the 'F' for Feature:

Analysed video systems for marketing.

Here is the 'A' for Analysis:

Analysed advanced video systems for computer orientated go-no-go decision for marketing.

Here is the 'B' for Benefit:

Analysed advanced video systems for computer orientated go/no-go decision for marketing, thereby giving technical approval for the company's most profitable product.

Listen to these:

'Reduced stock levels by 17.5 per cent, thereby releasing £210,000 into company cash flow.'

'Assisted in clients' understanding of VAT regulations thus improving customer relations.'

'Improved debt collection time from 85 to 54 days thus ensuring maximum cash flow.'

I'm sure you get the principle.

On pages 73–4 there are some 'Action words' to help you identify your achievements. Think about a job you have held, and put an 'I' in front of each action word to see if it triggers an achievement. Not all the words will generate achievements but a significant proportion should do so.

Chapter 25 Use the Past for the Future

Wherever possible, use the immediate past tense or 'aorist' form of the verb to introduce an achievement. The noun form or the participle form is not as powerful. (Don't worry, this is a book about CVs, not English grammar.)

Here are some examples:

'Managed' rather than 'the management'
'Improved' rather than 'the improvement'
'Investigated' rather than 'the investigation'

– i.e., the past tense rather than the noun.

And again:

'Designed' rather than 'designing'
'Analysed' rather than 'analysing'
'Directed' rather than 'directing'

– i.e., the past tense rather than the participle. The past tense gives the impression that you have actually done something. It is completed, it is finished, it is achieved – which on a CV is the impression you want to create.

Just two more things on achievements before we move on.

Deleting the first person 'I' makes it easier for you to give yourself proper credit without appearing overboastful.

By using the past tense you don't have to keep using 'I' because you can leave it out and replace it with an asterisk or star. The second point is that you can now indent your achievements on the page so that they stand out better and the eye of the reader is drawn towards them.

Here is an example:

Project Editor   Scholastic Digest   1990 – Present

Scholastic Digest is the largest publisher of scholastic material in the UK. My position was to manage the production of texts, magazines and multimedia instructional programmes for the sixth-form market. Main achievements:

★   Achieved product goals through supervision of staff ranging from 12 to 23 on projects up to £250,000, including independent copywriters and freelance editors
★   Conducted workshops for teachers so that . . .
★   Won the Miller education prize for . . .

Note here the order, job then company them employment dates. There is a brief description of the job followed by the achievements which are indented and the 'I' has been omitted.

Action words

ACHIEVED
ACQUIRED
ADMINISTERED
ADVISED
ANALYSED
ANTICIPATED
APPOINTED
APPRAISED
APPROVED
ARRANGED
ATTAINED
ASSESSED
AUDITED
AUGMENTED
AVERTED
AVOIDED
BOUGHT
BUILT
CAPTURED
CENTRALIZED
COMBINED
COMPLETED
COMPOSED
CONCEIVED
CONTROLLED
CONVERTED
CO-ORDINATED
CORRECTED
COUNSELLED

CREATED
DECREASED
DEFINED
DEMONSTRATED
DESIGNED
DETERMINED
DEVELOPED
DEVISED
DIRECTED
DOCUMENTED
DOUBLED
EDITED
EFFECTED
ELIMINATED
EMPLOYED
ENFORCED
ENGINEERED
ENSURED
ESTABLISHED
ESTIMATED
EVALUATED
EXCEEDED
EXECUTED
EXTRACTED
FORECAST
FORMED
FORMULATED
GENERATED
GUIDED

HIRED
IMPLEMENTED
IMPROVED
IMPROVISED
INCREASED
INITIATED
INSPIRED
INSPECTED
INSTIGATED
INSTRUCTED
INSURED
INTERPRETED
INTERVIEWED
INTRODUCED
INVENTED
INVESTIGATED
LAUNCHED
LED
LIAISED
LIGHTENED
LIQUIDATED
MAINTAINED
MANAGED
MARKETED
MODERNIZED
MONITORED
NEGOTIATED
OBTAINED
OPERATED

ORDERED
ORGANIZED
ORIGINATED
PERFORMED
SURVEYED
PIONEERED
PLANNED
POSITIONED
PREPARED
PRESENTED
PREVENTED
PROCESSED
PROCURED
PRODUCED
PROMOTED
PROVED
PROVIDED
PUBLISHED
PURCHASED
RECOMMENDED
RECRUITED

RECTIFIED
RE-DESIGNED
REDUCED
REGULATED
REJECTED
RELATED
REMEDIED
REORGANIZED
RESEARCHED
RESOLVED
REVAMPED
REVIEWED
REVISED
REVITALIZED
SAVED
SCHEDULED
SECURED
SELECTED
SIMPLIFIED
SOLD
SOLVED

SPECIFIED
STAFFED
STANDARDIZED
STIMULATED
STREAMLINED
STUDIED
SUPERVISED
SUPPORTED
SURPASSED
SURVEYED
TAUGHT
TERMINATED
TESTED
TIGHTENED
TRADED
TRAINED
TRANSLATED
TRIPLED
UTILIZED
VITALIZED
WROTE

Chapter 26 Rank Order

Having used the FAB and 'ed's, we are in a position to list our achievements. Well, not quite. Just one more point, and it is another strategy that comes straight from sales.

A rhyming couplet that all good salesmen know is this:

> *'If I can see the world through John Smith's eyes,*
> *I can sell John Smith what John Smith buys'*

Write for the reader

Apply this principle to your list of achievements. Looking at the list of all the things you have done, which do you think Mr Smith, the recruiter, would like to see first, second, third, etc? For example, as an advertising accounts executive you might be most proud of your creative copywriting skills and thus at the top of your achievement list is

Created concepts and wrote copy for . . .

but the job centres around good client management. This is what Mr John Smith is looking for.

So you should lead with

Successfully planned promotions for blue-chip clients

before giving any information about how creative your copywriting can be.

In rank ordering your CV, always write for the reader, our John Smith, and not for yourself.

Chapter 27 Tell Them What They Want To Know

Next important principle: Include only relevant information. If something does not support your career goal, then think hard about including it. Let me give you a personal example. I now work as a Chartered Psychologist with organizations large and small, and mainly work with clients on the resolution of management problems. My first job on leaving school was working in a gin factory in Stratford, London E15, stacking bottles. My second job was working as a lift-man in a treacle factory on the Barking Creek in East Ham. My third was as a kitchen hand in Plaistow, again in London. Now on my CV this information would be true, it might even be interesting, but it definitely would not be helpful.

Relevant information only

My CV therefore would say:

> *To enable self-funding through university a variety
> of casual jobs during the period 19—to 19—.*

I have only included relevant information.

We have seen CVs where people have given their Social
Security number, their passport number, medical card number
– all irrelevant.

Leave the children until later

Frequently on CVs one sees the full names of their children,
dates of birth and where they were born. When we challenged
the writer of such a CV he justified himself by saying: 'But wait,
the employer needed to know all this' – the answer is 'yes', but
not at the CV stage. Remember the maxim – only enough
information to get you the interview.

Chapter 28 Kids' Ages

Whilst talking about children – and this goes for men as well as women – if your children are at the ages 1, 2, 3, 5, 8, 10, 11, 13, 15 or 17, all those ages will ring alarm bells in the recruiter's mind because they are critical if a move or relocation to the new job is called for. The best place to explain what you are going to do about your children's education is at interview and then only if it is raised by the interviewer.

Grown up children

Also, if your age is outside the 'golden decade' don't say you have two children aged 25 and 27; it just emphasizes your age again. The recruiter who is just the gatekeeper might think to herself before she has even seen you 'Goodness, this person has children who are older than me.'

Chapter 29 No Jokes Please, Recruitment is Serious

Many people try to liven up the selector's day by injecting humour into their CVs. Don't be tempted. Don't be cute, chatty or funny. Selection and recruitment is a serious business. To be in the recruitment business is to be in a risk averse business like law or accounting – when it is easier for a recruiter to say 'No' than 'Yes', he or she usually says 'No'. By and large, recruiters always say 'No' to humour. Not because they are boring people but because their own jobs depend on how successful they are at picking the right people. What do you think happens to recruiters who keep selecting the wrong people? They join the job market very quickly.

It is difficult to be funny in person, let alone on paper.

Misfired humour

Here are some samples from people who have tried to be funny on their CVs. Under interests:

> *'Golf, golf and more golf'*

Now, I'm personally not a golfer so I'm not too impressed by that. Under reasons for leaving a job:

> *'To keep up with the school fees'*

Now, if I have strong views about equality and the benefits of state education, this is not going to find very much favour. Under main achievements:

> *'Wrestling with machine code and winning'*

If I'm looking for a programmer, I would expect this anyway.

Basic rule: Don't try to be funny. Your CV should be serious if you want your application to be taken seriously.

Chapter 30 Reasons for Leaving

Even in these days there is still an implicit understanding that people want and employers can provide lifetime employment. Maybe it is a hangover from the bygone age of the fifties and sixties when once you were employed by an organization you were there for life. Job hopping now as then was not thought to be good; it hints at instability.

The four reasons for leaving

Consequently, it is better not to include reasons for leaving on your CV. Such information can only serve to remind the potential employer that you are in control of your career rather than vice versa. Also, there are basically only four reasons why people leave jobs – better prospects, more pay, relocation or they were fired. Any of them, if the employer thinks about them seriously, makes you a potential risk as an employee – the question 'will you stay' is raised by the first three and the last will guarantee you stay unemployed. It is better to leave such things to be explained during the interview, than to try to justify your career moves at the CV stage.

How not to get an interview

The worst case we ever saw was on a CV that ran:

> *REASONS FOR LEAVING:*
> *Dismissed: Due to personality clash with boss:*
> *Currently taking this employer to an Industrial*
> *Tribunal: Confident of winning.*

He came to us wondering why his CV was not producing any interviews!

The advice is, leave out 'Reasons for leaving' from your CV. Explain it later in the selection process and then only on a specific invitation to do so by the interviewer.

Chapter 31 **Early Mistakes**

If you were once a junior secretary and are now a Director of Advertising or Human Resources Manager, it is not going to be helpful to put your early job on your CV. If you were a lab technician before you became an accountant, or took your law degree part time whilst working as a janitor, it just does not help to include the more humble positions.

Recent jobs only

Most employers are mainly interested in what you have been doing recently. What you did ten years ago is unlikely to make a significant contribution to your next job. So where appropriate use summary statements such as 'Prior to 19— a variety of junior jobs in engineering and retailing'. Note we mention the industries sector not the job titles.

Sometimes a previous job is directly useful and then it should be included: a meat buyer who was once a butcher, for example, or a nurse who is now a Unit General Manager are obvious examples of relevant experience. It was once said that the British car industry began to fail when accountants were appointed to run them rather than engineers who had shop floor experience.

You will have to decide for yourself how best to account for the early years of your career on your CV. The basic question to ask is: does it fit and/or support my present career aspirations? If it does not help you in any way, then it should be omitted.

Chapter 32 **Education**

Your education successes should be set out employing the same principles as in the career section. Please do not make your employer hack through all your GCSEs if you have a degree or higher qualification. Consequently, the reverse chronological rule applies just as much to education as it does to your career.

Obsolete degrees

In the same way your qualification is more important than where it was gained, which is more important again than when it was achieved. The number of CVs where the date of the qualification is given first is quite amazing. For those outside the 'golden decade' (see pages 26–7), this can only accentuate your age – 'Gosh, this person was at university before I was born!' Also, in today's world of rapid change most science degrees are obsolete in terms of usable knowledge after about a decade. What is being sold is not the things you know about but the intellectual, conceptual and analytical abilities which you demonstrated in order to gain the qualification.

The 'topsy curve'

What frequently occurs up to the age of 30 is what is called the 'Topsy CV', because it just grew. This is a graduate CV which was written on leaving university and then subsequently added to prior to each job move. Thus a 'Topsy CV' gives as much weight to the final year project at university or college as it does to the achievements of the last job. With a little thought it becomes obvious that newly qualified job seekers need to provide lots of information about their studies because they have nothing else to offer. Once someone has had some work experience the emphasis must shift to this area. Employers, except in academia and not always then, are more interested in what you can do for them than how well qualified you are. Sometimes this is difficult for the highly qualified to accept. Just ask yourself the question 'If I was about to be treated in an emergency, who would I prefer to undertake the operation – a recently qualified surgeon who had not performed the operation before, or a paramedic who had successfully completed the procedure many times?' The latter, of course. Ideally one would like qualifications together with the successful experience but given a choice, experience wins every time.

Resisting an education

This is why those without formal tertiary qualifications, if they have been successful in their careers, should not worry about not having degrees and diplomas. Employers prefer experience. Yes, of course, there are the professions where formal qualifications are a prerequisite for a job, but in the wide world of work, professional jobs are a small fraction of the total. In fact, although I would not recommend this as an excuse not to gain qualifications, most entrepreneurs from Alan Sugar to Richard Branson to the late Robert Maxwell seem to do rather well without the more traditional formal qualifications. Sometimes, it takes a good brain to resist an education!

To return again to your qualifications, your GCSEs, A levels or the courses you did at college. If you are pursuing a career in the sciences do not list your GCSEs thus:

English, English Literature, History, French, Geography, Maths, Chemistry and Physics

It is not as impressive as

Maths, Physics, Chemistry, etc.

The same principle can be applied to topics and projects at college – lead with the most appropriate first.

Chapter 33 # Health

Should you tell your prospective employer about your state of health? You could take the view that how healthy you are is your own private concern. But it is obvious that the employer wants employees who are at work rather than off work with some malady and drawing sick pay. Consequently, if you are healthy, say so, for it can only be in your favour. 'Excellent' is the word which most frequently appears on CVs, though I am not sure of the difference between good health and excellent health.

If your health has not been good then my advice is not to say so on the CV. The fact that you are returning to work must mean that you are currently fit for work, but this is the sort of information which is far better discussed at interview. If I have two candidates whose CVs offer the same skills and experience, but one candidate confesses a significant health problem from which he has fully recovered and the other does not (although he too suffered from the same illness), it is obvious which one will be given preference for the interview.

An illusion of good health

A way of creating the illusion of good health is to include some reference to a sporting activity among your interests and, if possible, a sporting achievement, no matter how long ago. It shows that you were fit and healthy at one time in your life with the implication that you are still fit now.

Employers are, for obvious reasons, biased against the weak and the sick, no matter how fit they are now. The best place to justify your fitness for the job is at the interview, not at the CV stage. So if you are healthy say so; if not, then omit this information.

Where disability is a plus

The exception is if you are registered disabled. In my experience employers positively discriminate in favour of those who used to be called 'green card carriers'. If your disability does not have a direct bearing on your job, then it is almost a guarantee of an interview.

If you have an obvious disability my advice would be, whether or not you declared it on your CV, to advise your potential employer before you go for the interview. If you attend interviews in a wheelchair or have a false limb and this has not been mentioned on the CV it is likely that you will be remembered for your disability rather than the skills and experience you can bring to the job irrespective of your suitability.

Chapter 34 Special CVs

Netting Jobs

The potential of the World Wide Web or Internet to gain jobs is huge in its pros and cons.

Currently in the US more than half the jobs available are filled via the Internet and the UK is not that far behind with many firms only accepting applications that are e-mailed.

However surfer beware !!!!!
The Internet is only an additional route to a job and it is not easy to navigate for a host of reasons.

★   Your personal information is more public. You cannot always update your information

★ You do not know how long your information is available for

★ You don't know who has access to your information

Then there is the search side. On January 1, 2000 by doing a general search on suitable topics you would get the following:

Search	Number of sites found
'Jobs'	4,162,829
'Career+Jobs'	6,260
'Graduate+Jobs'	1,200

So you would need to go to a filter or gateway site which will do much of the culling of your information for you.

There are several out there such as:

http://www.lifestyle.co.uk

for general information and list of agencies, although it is for graduates:

http://www.prospects.csu.man.ac.uk

is very helpful, as is

http//www.jobs4grads.co.uk

You should also know that some search engines have their own career and job sections which work as gateway sites; for example go to:

www.yahoo.com/Business/Employment/

To actually find a job similar to using an agency there are many sites available to give you a flavour. Go to:

http://www.taps.co.uk/graduate-jobs-uk.htm

Putting it together:

If you need guidance on how to put together an electronic CV then American sites currently offer the best advice. Go to:

http://jobsmart.org/tools/resume/res-elec.htm

for some excellent tips.

Information on potential employers? Work through:

http://www.dunandbrad.co.uk/homepage/index.htm

For jobs in Europe you might like to try:

www.europayer.com

If you draw a blank on your search engine then try

http://www.metacrawler.com/

which will give you access to a variety of search engines, including AltaVista, Excite, Infoseek, LookSmart, Lycos, The Mining Co, Thunderstone and, of course, Yahoo.

One of the advantages of the post is that your CV can arrive in the form that you wish with the appropriate fonts, spacing and bolding you have chosen to show yourself off to the best advantage. When your beautiful CV is converted to standard

ASCII by e-mail it has the same effect as a school uniform – suddenly yours looks the same as everyone else's. This has a significant implication for and a greater emphasis on content which really does have to be better than all those competitors.

Also if your prospective employer does not have the same page set-up, even if you send your CV as an attachment the result can be a travesty.

It is a good idea to send your CV to a few friends to see how it comes out and then make the appropriate changes. Follow up with a hard copy.

The sensible person might add a sentence at the end of their CV or covering letter such as:

'If you e-mail me by return I would be delighted to send you an appropriate formatted copy of my CV by post so that my details are printed properly.'

Gimmick CVs

Do not be tempted to use gimmicks. If your CV needs a special gimmick to gain attention, rather than your achievements or skills, then although your CV will be noticed it will not pass closer scrutiny.

If your CV is markedly different in paper colour or typeface it says quietly, 'I'm an outsider trying to get in.' A gimmick CV gives the same message even more clearly.

The CV and the rail pass

Successful exceptions are few. A gimmick CV that worked was for a traineeship in the creative department of a famous PR and advertising company. Here the applicant did a one-page CV, had it miniaturized and gummed to the back of a weekly rail travel pass, and sent it with a one-line covering letter which read,

Look what you can have if you fund one of these each week.

It gained an interview and the job. An Asian graduate trainee wrote off to all the recruiters that were visiting his university offering himself as an Indian take-away with his qualification, skills and experience set out like a menu for an Indian meal. Again, this worked, but by and large gimmick CVs provide a little welcome humour and diversion in the recruiter's humdrum day and little else. Would you buy a car because of flashing lights in the show window or select a restaurant for a celebration dinner because of the chance of winning a weekend break away? Like you, employers are essentially traditional and sensible in their buying habits and not influenced by the superficial. Keep your CV normal.

Disk CV

If you want a computing job in a small or high-tech company, putting your CV on a disk used to be a popular approach which began, like so many of these things, in the US. However, since the advent of computer viruses many firms have strict policies about the use of disks when their pedigree and form are unknown.

Chapter 35 Coping with Bias

Recruitment is unfair. Yes, there is some legislation designed to minimize discrimination against applicants for reasons of sex, race, colour or creed but a lot of prejudices still exist.

The basic rule is to put any information which ignorant, prejudiced people will use against you on the back page. If you are not British don't put your nationality immediately after your name and address. It just does not help. If you have a foreign sounding name yet you look British, then use a photograph irrespective of my advice on page 38.

Changing your name

I worked with a beautiful and brilliant Ethiopian woman who graduated from Oxford University with a good honours degree. She was fluent in English, French and Italian as well as several dialects of her homeland. The facts are these. She sent 150 CVs to graduate recruiters and had no invitations to interview. She anglicized her name and remailed the 150 CVs and achieved 10 interviews. There were only two variables – her name and the time she sent her CV.

In the UK you can choose to call yourself by any name you wish providing it is not your intention to defraud. Maybe John Smith and Fred Bloggs are having a hard time and a zero response from their CVs which they are circulating in Ethiopia.

The vexed question of marital status

We were recently working as consultants with a young woman who held very strong feminist views, she objected to putting her marital status on her CV. In the end we persuaded her to do 50 CVs with her status and 50 without. I regret to report that it was the latter that generated more interviews. We have repeated the experiment several times since and achieved the same response.

It is a difficult decision. If one has to go to these lengths to get a job with a company, would you really want to work for that company anyway?

Chapter 36 What to Leave Out

As the CV will form the basis of the interview, and negative information at interview always attracts more supplementary and probing questions, your CV should contain only that which is positive about you. So here is a section about what you might like to leave out. Of course, you must be prepared to answer questions in these areas at interview, but at the CV stage your maxim should be:

'Yours to know and theirs to find out.'

Avoiding prejudice

Remember that each of us at a basic level is biased. Birds of a feather flock together and recruiters are no different from the rest. They like to recruit in their own image. Most recruiters in the UK are WASPS – that is, white, Anglo-Saxon and Protestant. They are also married with 2.3 children, living in suburbia and able to buy their clothes from M&S. If you are different in any way from the norm then the sorry fact of life is that you will experience prejudice at the CV paper sort. Things are, fortunately, changing but we have not yet had many prime ministers with few O levels who spend some of their years in Brixton. If it is a fact that recruiters are biased then do not give them the opportunity to exercise this inadequacy at the CV sort stage. Any information which can give rise to bias should be left out. It is an indictment of our present society but if you are single, black, an ex-shop steward who failed your Bar finals at the first attempt and spent five years 15 years ago working for London Transport, are politically active, jailed for civil disobedience and have dual Nigerian/UK citizenship your chances of getting to interview for a typical law job if you include this information are slim, irrespective of how brilliant your career and achievements may be.

Suggested omissions

Here are some things you might like to consider omitting:

(Those marked with an asterisk * are dealt with specifically elsewhere in the book.)

★ Examinations you have failed
★ Your health, if poor*
★ Major illness, both physical and mental*
★ Junior jobs irrelevant to your present career thrust*
★ Employment of less than a year

- ★ Reason for leaving employment*
- ★ Dates of qualifications
- ★ Ages of children*
- ★ Marital Status – if female*
  - – if gay
  - – if single and over 30
- ★ Children, if adult*
- ★ Period(s) of state detention
- ★ Past Trade Union status – unless you are going for a job in industrial relations with a Union or in politics
- ★ Dangerous or 'different' interests, e.g., hand-gliding and bungie jumping
- ★ Nationality if not British – securing work permits is extra unwanted and difficult work for employers
- ★ Political affiliations
- ★ Place of birth if not in UK
- ★ Fluency in languages of no direct use within the Western world or to the job on offer
- ★ Higher qualifications if the jobs for which you are applying have no need of them
- ★ Your current salary and benefits*
- ★ Your anticipated salary and benefits*
- ★ Your photograph*
- ★ Your referees*
- ★ Your career ambitions/objectives unless you are a recent graduate
- ★ Anything that makes you look extreme or different

Chapter 37 But I've Already Sent Out My CV to Lots of Employers

Do not worry if you have bought this book after sending out your CV, because CVs have a shelf life of at most about two weeks in the mind of recruiters. Your CV might get put in the potential candidates file but either way you can always send it again on the pretext of having updated the document for the employer. Many a time in my experience an employer has seen a candidate on the 'new improved' CV whereas there was a nil response to the original document.

Chapter 38 CV Don'ts – Again

★ Do not list your last salary or your salary requirement.
★ Do not disclose why you have left your previous jobs.
★ Do not list addresses of the firms you have worked for.
★ Do not give the names or job titles of the people you worked for.
★ Do not use 'I' unless really necessary.
★ Do not use jargon.
★ Do not use abbreviations which will not be understood by all the potential recipients of your CV.
★ Do not have any spelling or grammatical errors.
★ Do not send photocopies.
★ Do not send cheap paper.
★ Do not use extreme type faces, silly visual effects or a brochure format.
★ Do not include a photograph.

Chapter 39 Application Forms

You will find it very frustrating if having spent hours on crafting your CV and sending it off with the perfect covering letter, the only reward for your labours is an application form.

Whilst this may he frustrating, remember two things. First, not everyone gets an application form so your CV has done its job. Second, no application form I have yet seen gives the applicant scope to write everything that is appropriate. This means your CV can still play its important role in gaining the interview.

How recruiters use them

Employers use application forms rather like the army uses uniforms – they position everyone. It is easier for recruiters to interview from an application form because they know where to look for what they want, whether it be experience, personal details or expertise. It is helpful when you are trying to keep up the rapport to be able to glance down to a certain position and know that that section on the form will give the required information. Hacking through a CV at interview mitigates against rapport and a natural flow to the conversation.

For further information . . .

Employers will not shortlist you if you return the application form over which you have printed, however neatly, PLEASE SEE CV. You must complete the form: but in doing so you can write at the bottom of various sections particularly those detailing experience and achievements FOR FURTHER INFORMATION PLEASE SEE MY CV, which, of course, you have enclosed. (Please do not expect employers to have kept your previous CV or documentation.) It is no guarantee that your CV will be read again but you have given it your best shot.

Chapter 40 # What Next?

Once the CV has been written it must find its way to as many appropriate desks as possible. It is surprising that so many people spend ages constructing their CV and then don't send it to anyone, as if the invitations are supposed to come by some form of osmosis.

Learning to 'pyramid'

To whom should you send your CV? Here you have to learn to pyramid – as in pyramid sales. Your CV needs to go to someone who:

1   Can offer you a job
2   Refer you to someone who can offer you a job
3   Can tell you of a job opening

4 Refer you to someone who can suggest a potential job
5 Can give you the name of someone who can do any of the above

THERE IS NO LIMIT

Getting a job is a process of being turned down. Getting an interview is about telling as many people as possible that you are looking for the next stage in your career. If your CV stays on your desk at home, so will your career.

Chapter 41 Who Can Give You a Job

'Spend as much time as you can with prospective customers' is a basic rule of sales. Salesmen who spend all their time at their desk writing reports, talking to their design and manufacturing people and generally staying in house are unlikely to be successful because none of those people is likely to buy their product. It is the same for the job hunter – who is going to give you a job? It is not

Family – they can give you support

or

Friends – they can maybe tell you of openings

or

Agencies – they can only submit your details on your behalf or

Personnel Departments – they can only shortlist you.

It is only decision makers in appropriate firms that can give you the job you want.

Picking up the £50 notes

If an eccentric millionaire passed you on the street scattering handfuls of £50, £20, £10 and £5 notes there would soon be lots of people, including yourself, picking up the paper money. The best strategy would be not to pick up as many notes as possible but to collect as many of the high denominations as you could. In this way you would maximize the gains. Job search should follow the same principles. Most people just write to agencies then sit back and complain that

a) they have heard nothing
b) agencies and head hunters are hopeless
c) agencies cannot understand your technical expertise

(although the latter might make you feel good when you have just had your ego dented by needing to change jobs). It is only employers who can give someone a job, so they are the equivalent of the £50 notes. Of course, your letter will be regarded as junk mail by most of them but you are more likely to be successful here than working with the other categories (the lower denominations in cash terms).

John Courtis, who runs his own excellent head hunting

firm, sends a standard letter to job searchers – it makes the point so well that I have set it out in full on page 140.

The moral is simple: *Spend most of your energy contacting the most likely employers.*

Chapter 42 Covering Letter

Remember the sum on page 13. Not only does it apply to the CV but also to the covering letter. In fact more so, because the covering letter is the packaging for the CV. If the letter does not command the attention of the selector then why should he or she go on to read the CV?

Here are some obvious basics.

First, where possible it should be typed. Most written business communications are typed; if your letter is not you are signalling quite clearly to your future employer that you are an outsider trying to get in.

Don't split the infinitives!

Of course spelling and grammar should both be correct. Split infinitives still annoy people. You must remember that at this stage in the selection process it is only your letter and CV that contain information about you and who wants an employee who cannot even present him or herself correctly?

I would suggest that you do not right-hand justify your letter. As with the CV, it gives the impression that this is a standard document (which, of course, it is) that you have sent off to hundreds of potential employers (which, of course, you have).

See Chapter 44 for further advice on letters.

Chapter 43 To Whom?

Your letter must go to a named person. 'Dear Sir Madam' is an insult. Until you secure the interview your letter has the status of junk mail. If you begin 'Dear Sir/Madam' it is more likely to be treated as such, and will probably not even reach the decision maker. Secretaries are paid to file junk or unsolicited mail vertically under W.B. If the Reader's Digest can reach you by name and personalize the correspondence, you can do the same, so write directly to the likely decision maker by name.

Finding the right name

The decision maker is likely to be your potential boss's boss. It is usually quite easy to find out the name of the appropriate recipient just by telephoning the receptionist. Some organizations, like banks, pharmaceutical companies and defence organizations have policies about not giving information over the telephone, in which case go to one of the directories (in any reference library), find the appropriate director and ask them or their secretary. Tell them that you want to send some information to the person responsible for the xyz function, would it be the director (or his/her secretary) to whom you are speaking? This usually prompts a 'No' and that it should go to Mr or Miss so-and-so.

If you are a director or a senior executive then write to the Chief Executive by name. They are probably inundated with unsolicited mail from job hunters but if you have a skill profile which might be useful they will respond appropriately. The letters on pages 137 and 138 are real examples and proof that the system works.

The personnel department

Giving you this advice will alienate my friends in personnel and human resources departments. Being responsible for recruitment and selection, they naturally expect all job hunters' correspondence to be directed to them. However, good and professional as they are, personnel departments are but gate-keepers, albeit important gatekeepers, in the selection process. Personnel selectors can only say 'No', they cannot say 'Yes'. It would not be fair to talk about monkeys and organ grinders, buttons and shirts or oily rags and engineers, but the principle is the same. It is only if you want a job in personnel or human resources that you should write to that department, important though it is. Always write to the person who can give you a job.

THE EXAMPLES Covering Letters

The Best Job-Hunt Book in the World

Chapter 44 Structure of the Covering Letter

The purpose of the covering letter is very simple: it is to get the recipient to read your CV – no more, no less. Although this is obvious and simplistic, it is surprising how many covering letters

★ Are too long
★ Repeat the content of the CV
★ Are written from the applicant's point of view
★ Contain negative information

and besides all this contain spelling and grammatical errors.

To my mind and in my experience, the covering letter needs only three paragraphs.

1st Paragraph From the recipient's viewpoint or benefit give your reason for writing.

A good way of ensuring this is to use the sales letter strategy of beginning this paragraph with the word 'Your'.

For example:

★ 'Your advertisement was of great interest . . .'
★ 'Your company enjoys an excellent reputation in engineering . . .'
★ 'Your article in *Business Week* . . .'
★ 'Your recent results . . .'

Employers are bound to be interested in what is happening from their viewpoint.

2nd Paragraph To customize your CV and direct the reader to some unique selling point which meets or hits a specific need of the potential employer.

For example:

★ 'You will see from my enclosed CV . . .'
★ 'Customer Services has been the main thrust of my career . . .'
★ 'Last year I won the largest widget order in the North East . . .'
★ 'Being a Unix specialist who is fluent in German . . .'

3rd Paragraph This is to ask for the interview, although interviews are work for personnel people. So we translate this into 'discussion' or 'meeting'.

For example:

★ 'The opportunity of a discussion . . .'
★ 'The chance to meet with you . . .'

Finally, this third paragraph is to prompt the reader into some form of action, thus:

★ 'I look forward to hearing from you'

or, if you are applying for jobs where some degree of confidence and assertiveness is required or expected:

★ 'Perhaps I may telephone your office next week to see how you may wish to progress the matter . . .'

You will notice that this is the first and only place where tentative language is used, 'Perhaps I may . . .', 'to see how you may wish . . .' This just takes the aggressive edge off the intention. For the most part, with cold letters your call will not be welcome but in today's climate no one will think ill of you if you work hard at getting a job. Remember, if there is a potential position for you your call will be welcome.

You will find examples of how to end your letter in Chapter 45.

What follows are some tips and strategies and what not to do in the Covering Letter and some suggestions as to how they could be improved. We begin with three examples of what not to do.

Example 1 – what not to do

16 Quartz Close
Woosehill
Wokingham
Berkshire
RG11 9TS

26 May 1992

Dear Sir/Madam,

I have seen your advertisements in various publications and feel that you are ideally placed to help me further my career.

I am an experienced Computer Customer Service Professional, and I currently work for one of the leading companies in the field. I am looking to expand my experience by moving to another company.

I would welcome an opportunity to discuss my experience and any potential opportunities with you. I will call you next week.

Yours sincerely,

Mr P.1. Maxin

Comments

From someone who is in customer service this is dreadful. Here are some of the errors:

1 'Dear Sir/Madam' – This is almost saying, 'I don't care who you are and I'm too lazy to find out.'
2 Every sentence begins with 'I' – the writer sounds like an 'ego' maniac.
3 The whole letter is written from the viewpoint of what the

potential employer can do for the applicant. In retailing terms this letter is almost the equivalent of a shopkeeper putting up a sign in his window saying, 'Shop here so I can make a profit on you.'

4   'I will call you next week' – There is a difference between assertiveness which is essential in getting a job these days and naked aggression. This bald statement is just rude!!

5   'Yours sincerely' – You must get this right. Dear Sir demands a 'Yours faithfully'. Only when writing to a specifically named person is 'Yours sincerely' appropriate.

6   'Mr P.1. Maxin' – he *must* be an egoist. It is not customary to put the appellation Mr (or Ms, Mrs etc.) in front of your name. If you must do it, then put it after your name in brackets.

Example 2 – again, what not to do

Dear

I write in reference to our recent telephone conversation.

I enclose my CV for your consideration. I am aware that its presentation is not ideal and I am working on an improved format.

I have enjoyed a successful career in Engineering, including management, training, counselling and sales/marketing activities.

I am interested in the possibility of becoming an associate in such fields as . . .

Comments

This was a letter sent to our consultancy. It was hand-written and was not at all easy to read.

1   Ideally your covering letter should enjoy the same style and typeface as your CV. If this is not possible then do try to have it typed. If it is handwritten, since most of the world of work communicates on paper by the typed word, your letter signals clearly that you are an outsider trying to get in.

2   'I am aware that [my CV] is not ideal' – This is amazing! What is the implication here?
    – I can't be bothered to update it
    – You are not worth the effort of the rewrite
    – This application is less important than other things I have to do
    It would have been better not to allude to the paucity of the CV than include this statement.

3   'I have enjoyed a successful career' -implications of this should be thoroughly thought through. This phrase implies

to me that the writer is now retired and no longer making a positive or significant contribution.

4   '. . . in the possibility of . . . in such fields as . . .' Instructions on how to write sales letters make a significant point about tentative language. In covering letters it makes you sound unsure or uncertain. Phrases and words such as the following might usefully be omitted:

- I feel
- I think
- I might
- Perhaps
- Only
- Just
- It may

Unless, of course, you deliberately wish to appear tentative (see comment number 4 in Example 1).

Example 3 – this is the worst example

Dear Mr

Here are five reasons why you should employ me:

1   If you do not, one of your competitors will.
2   Leadership qualities, both verbally and by example.
3   A refusal to accept second-best in life.
4   Major achievements, mostly in the future.
5   In possession of a healthy body and a healthy mind.

Comments
In fact, the original had 11 reasons and the above represents an abbreviated version.

There is nothing wrong in making your covering letter different or being assertive or pushy but this is just silly, coming as it does from an MBA student. Even the points are open to question, for example:
1   What is a verbal leader?
2   How can you sell future achievements if you have no track record?
3   Employers take as read that employees are healthy.

This list could be offered by most applicants. There is little which is unique here. If you wish to try this approach, which sometimes works, then a strong client orientation, coupled with creative and individual uniqueness is a must.

Now for some better examples of what you should do.

Example 4

Dear

Engineering costs are a significant overload. For appropriate control, good management and best manufacturing methods are vital.

May I help in this important area?

My extensive skills and experience cover:

★ Engineering management in 'blue-chip' companies
★ Planning and executing capital investment programmes up to £2.3M
★ Reducing labour costs in a Trade Union environment
★ Introducing effective machine maintenance

The opportunity to discuss with you how my knowledge and ability could be used to your advantage would be most welcome.

Yours sincerely

Comments

This letter, which was sent cold to possible employers, won an interview and subsequently a job, so the letter did what it was supposed to do.

1 Notice how this letter, in comparison to Example 3, continually has the needs of the employer in mind and uses tentative language in the right place to soften the assertiveness.

2   The letter begins strongly with a statement which every manufacturing company would support.
3   Personally, I would have strengthened the selling points by:
    a) Using the past, e.g., Plann*ed* and execut*ed*
    b) Quantifying the reduction in labour costs and the machine maintenance
    c) Made more of the potential benefits to the employer.

Next is an example of how to present a non-traditional career.

Example 5

Dear

What do sweets and lighting have in common?

★ BOTH NEED TO DELIVER MAXIMUM CONSUMER SATISFACTION
★ BOTH NEED THEIR BENEFITS COMMUNICATED TO THEIR TARGET MARKETS
★ BOTH NEED TO GENERATE A SATISFACTORY PROFIT FOR THE COMPANY
★ BOTH HAVE BENEFITED FROM MY DIRECTION

As an experienced Marketing Director, I have a proven record in the management of change, resulting in increased customer satisfaction and an improved company profitability. My CV which is enclosed demonstrates this.

I am happy to supply further information or meet for a discussion when examples of my achievement can be matched more closely to situations in your organizations.

Yours sincerely

Comments

This is another cold letter to target employers.

1   This job seeker makes an advantage of a career background which is not normal, i.e., from confectionery to lighting products, in an interesting way.

2   The offer of 'examples of my achievements' is also an

additional reason why an employer might want to see you. You obviously have more chance of getting the job even if the interviewer initially only wants to see you because of your 'examples'.

Example 6 – letter to headhunter

Dear

    There is a legend that memories only last three months. I contacted you in the summer and am enclosing another copy of my CV to update your records.

    I would like to convert this piece of paper into a face and look forward to meeting you.

Yours sincerely,

Comments

This gained several interviews when the first CV, which was written before the writer had advice, achieved a nil response.

1   Headhunters receive hundreds of cold letters a day. They usually begin with a very boring 'I was a senior executive with . . .', so you can see how this effort was refreshingly different.
2   The last paragraph here is really interesting and provocative and I can see why it worked.
3   Most job seekers think that headhunters and agencies have hundreds of jobs on their books – they don't. Yes, they do use their contacts to secure assignments, but most of them do what most job seekers should be doing for themselves: contacting employers direct. My advice is be your own headhunter, representing yourself.

Headhunters, however, receive hundreds of unsolicited letters each week. See the advice of John Courtis in Chapter 47.

Example 7 – in response to an advert

Dear

The ability to steer the xxx Co. through an increasingly more complex and competitive marketplace.

The experience to understand intimately the requirements and opportunities for commercial sponsorship of the arts.

The stature to lead a prestigious organization and represent the xxx Co. at the highest levels of Industry and Government.

The skills to position the xxx Co. for optimum and profitable success.

The creative sensitivity to balance the artistic and the commercial requirements of the xxx Co.

If my understanding of the requirements for the role of Managing Director of the xxx Co. is correct, then you will find I certainly fit the bill! My attached CV details the bare bones of the success I have built as Managing Director and as President of the Industry Federation.

I look forward to an early opportunity to demonstrate how my particular skills and experience could be used to build and sustain the success of the xxx Co.

Oh yes! I trust that boundless energy and enthusiasm combined with an all consuming passion for classical music would not count against me?

Yours sincerely

Comments

This was written to a leading orchestra company in response to an advertisement.

1   The writer has attempted to get behind the words of the

advert to demonstrate that, although his background is in a totally different arena, he can identify the issues and has the skill and experience to address them.

2   The last line just hints at the disposition of the man behind the letter. (He did not get the job but he got an interview, although there were hundreds of applicants.)

3   In the original letter there was one split infinitive and one typo, but in this case the writer was forgiven.

Example 8

Dear Mr

Your paper machine quality control systems and distributed control systems have been formidable competitors to our products in South East Asia and Japan for several years now.

I have for some time been expecting the same competition from your excellent company in Europe and it is interesting to note that you are not more active in the European paper markets than you are.

Should your strategy be entering the European market for paper machine control systems I can be of direct assistance.

As you will see from my attached career résumé I helped establish Accuracy as the leading supplier of quality control systems to the paper industry in Europe and have in-depth knowledge and experience of this market in the UK, France, Holland, Belgium and Germany, as well as being trilingual.

My more recent experience includes the introduction of both the xx and yy Master systems to the paper and other industries.

Mr W. W., President of ZZ Corporation, who is a long-standing friend and colleague from the days when we worked together at BBB, suggests I write to you direct.

Perhaps I may telephone you in the next few days to determine when a convenient meeting can be arranged for us to discuss the opportunities which the European Market presents for you and the start-up assistance I could provide.

I do hope a brief meeting will be possible.

Yours sincerely

Comment

This was a cold letter. It did not gain a job but it did gain for this very able executive a two-week consultancy assignment in Japan.

Do your potential employers' thinking for them. This is an excellent example of an applicant who has done a wonderful job of doing his potential employer's thinking for him and then sold himself as the ideal candidate.

Chapter 45 Example Endings

It is surprising how many job hunters have difficulty ending their letters. Here are some examples, all of which come from letters that have won interviews:

★ I would be pleased to meet you to discuss how I could contribute to your organization.
★ I would welcome the opportunity to discuss with you how my knowledge and ability could be used in your company.
★ I hope there might be an opportunity for a personal discussion.
★ This letter and my CV provide the basis of my career achievements, but I would be pleased to flesh them out at a personal meeting to see if there is an opportunity to work with your company.
★ I am frequently in Cheltenham and can be contacted on 071-923 3456.

★ If you think it would help, I would be delighted to meet you, to talk about this.

★ My CV is enclosed. I would welcome a letter or your call to my office.

★ I live locally and would be pleased to discuss with you, at any time convenient to yourself, the position advertised or any other that will enable me to provide input and benefit to your organization.

★ I attach a note summarizing my background and experience. I should, of course, be glad to come and see you. May I ring to find out if a meeting could be worthwhile?

★ A phone call to my office (071-923 3456) will reach me, or a letter to the above address. My CV is attached. I hope to hear from you.

★ My CV is attached and if you would like to see me I should very much like to see you.

★ Might not do any harm, at least to talk, if you have a mind to. My CV is enclosed and I hope to hear from you.

★ I look forward to your reply and if there are any work areas upon which you require further information do not hesitate to contact me.

★ The broadly based interests I have developed would quickly allow me to raise my knowledge to specialist level in a number of fields – a bold statement but one you might be satisfied with if we would meet.

★ If I may, I will call your secretary next week to see if it is convenient for me to see you.

★ I would like to meet you so that I can elaborate on these bare facts and answer any questions. I look forward to hearing from you.

Chapter 46 Do Cold Letters Work?

Put simply – yes when sent to the people who can give you jobs – i.e., Employers. The best analogy I can give is that of oranges: everyone has bought oranges at some time. Greengrocers always display their fruit in the window or outside. Hundreds of people walk by every day and some purchase oranges. However, everybody needs oranges at some time. Job applicants should send out their CVs to anyone who might be able to offer them a job. Just as the greengrocer displays his oranges in front of potential purchasers, you should do the same with your CV. The grocer might hope that everyone will buy his oranges but he is not surprised or disappointed when people don't. Job seekers should have the same outlook.

On the following letters are extracts, with names which have been disguised, from actual letters leading to an interview which was gained from a cold application. Good covering letters do work!

Extract 1

Polymers Europe Ltd
Sutton
Surrey

2 April 1992

Mr James
5 Navarino Grove
Dalston
E8 1AJ

Dear Mr James

Many thanks for your recent letter and enclosed CV. As I am sure you are well aware, we do not currently have any vacancies at the moment, but nevertheless I have circulated your documents around some of our key managers, and should there be any relevance in talking to you, then you can be assured that we will follow up your approach to us.

Yours sincerely

Miss Cathy Admin

pp James Bigman
Managing Director

Extract 2

Polymers Europe Ltd
Sutton
Surrey

10 April 1992

Mr James
5 Navarino Grove
Dalston
E8 1AJ

Dear Mr James

Further to my letter dated 2nd April 1992, the comments of my colleagues are that we do not have any suitable opportunities for you at BBB. However, we are quite impressed by your skills profile and it occurs to us that this may be of interest to one of our associated companies Polymer Chemicals at Southampton. I have, therefore, passed your papers on to them.

Yours sincerely

James Bigman
Managing Director

Chapter 47 A Headhunter Speaks

What follows is a letter from John Courtis of John Courtis & Partners Search and Selection. The letter was sent in response to a cold call to his firm. What John Courtis says makes such sense that the letter, with his permission, appears in full.

Dear

Thank you for your letter and CV. None of our current assignments matches your background and experience. Nonetheless we'll keep your CV on file with pleasure.

However, I am not sure that we are likely to be much use to you. What you have gained is entry to a sort of lottery. The reality of our existence is that we react to what our clients ask us to do. We can't predict what that is likely to be, even for a record like yours.

If you consider the criteria attached to any search or selection assignment you'll recognise that there are almost endless permutations of industry, sector, qualification, age, experience, location and so on. Actually, we receive over ten thousand applications per year but only handle a few hundred jobs.

Add to this the fact that our client list is finite and we are one of many consultancies providing recruitment services, so the odds against a perfect match with you are long. We'd love to help; if only because, when you've got a new job, we hope you may become our client.

My colleague, John McManus, tends to offer ancient wisdom on these occasions. Tell them to write to people who've got jobs to offer, he cries – they're called employers. He doesn't put it prettily, but he's right. Targeting Chief Executives within your area of competence is likely to be more productive. After all, if a job doesn't exist and they like what you say, they can invent one. We cannot.

Yours sincerely,

John Courtis, FCA, MPIM

P.S. Despite what some advisers say, we would appreciate an indication of your last salary. There are both practical and statutory reasons for this. You can tell us what lesser sum you'd accept too, if it's appropriate.

The Best Job-Hunt Book in the World

Chapter 48 The Structure of the CV

There are some traditions and expectations about the structure of CVs, but it is more important that you develop a structure which shows off you and your talents to their best advantage.

The traditional structure, popularly known as 'tombstone', is as follows:

Name
Address
Telephone number
Date of Birth
Marital status and children
Interests/Health
Secondary education
Tertiary education
Professional qualifications

Employment history
(in chronological order)

Our Consultancy has not found this structure as successful as:

Name
Address
Telephone Number
Career Statement
Career and Achievements to date
(in reverse chronological order)
Professional qualifications and training
Tertiary education
Secondary education
Interests
Personal details

We think this structure achieves more interviews because it delivers information to the potential employer in the order that it is required to make the decision whether or not to interview.

Qualifications

Employers are going to be more interested in what you can do in terms of skill and experience before you tell them how old you are or indeed what your interests are. We advocate, for those with recognized and job-relevant qualifications, that these are put after the individual's name on the basis that the employer can see immediately that you are a graduate or that you enjoy an appropriate professional qualification. The education section can then go after your career because the reader already knows what you have achieved in this area.

There is an old adage that it takes 'a good brain to resist an education'. If you have made it to a senior position through a rigorous education in the university of life and hard knocks, then leave the education section out altogether. As we have said elsewhere, employment is about what you can do for an employer and not about how many certificates you can put up on the office wall.

A question of age

However, this suggestion of leaving things out does not apply to age. If you are over 60 then you still have to declare your age. If it is absent, employers, in our experience, guess the reason for your omission and it draws attention to something that you obviously perceive as a problem – otherwise why would you have left it out in the first place?

What follows are some examples of various types of CVs. Some much better than others. Please use them as guides where appropriate and do not be tempted to copy. In our experience, applicants who crib chunks from the CVs of others have greater difficulty with their interviews: they have problems substantiating other people's achievements!

Example 1: what not to do

Curriculum Vitae

Name: David John Applicant
Address: 15 Buckingham Gardens Highwood
               London E8 1AJ

Telephone:	071-923 3456
Date of Birth:	4th April 1946
Place of Birth:	Norbury, South London
Nationality:	British
Marital Status:	Married
Children:	Two aged 10 girl
	14 boy
House:	Owner
Car:	Owner/Driver
Passport:	Holder
Interests:	Music/Photography, Film making, Mountaineering, Sound Equipment

Qualifications

1963 GCE. 0 Levels. English Language, English Literature, Mathematics, Science, and Technical Drawing.

1968 Ordinary National Certificate, Electronics and General Engineering (Sutton College).

1969 Apprenticeship with Kent Transformers Ltd with part sandwich degree course at N.E.L. Polytechnic.

1976 Digital Electronics Engineering Course, High Power Ltd, London.

1980 Analogue Data Analysis Short Course, Johnson Ltd, Frimley.

1983 Data Signal Processing Seminar, Monologic Ltd.

1986 Management Training Course, XXX Ltd, (Brighton Polytechnic).

Industrial experience 1974 to 1979

Project Engineer

Optic Power Ltd, Chertsey, Surrey

– Trouble-shooting on site at the Strand Theatre, of Scenery

Hoist Control Systems. Including Analogue computing and 415 Volt, 6 Phase Thyrister drive systems.

- Customer presentations and Systems training. Including Digital computing and power drives.
- Specialist power servo products Site Engineer. Including on site problem diagnosis and customer liaison.
- RAF Shoreham, Aircraft wind tunnel development and site engineer. Including Installation Commissioning and testing of computer controlled 415 volt 3 phase drive systems.

1979 to 1985

Principal Systems Engineer/Project Manager
Exim Command and Control Systems Ltd, Croydon, Surrey

- Overall responsibility for up to twelve engineers.
- Management of Control System development (systems, real time software, and servo engineering).
- General Systems Engineering. Including planning of trials and controlling a team to analyse results.
- Systems Engineering enhancement programme to introduce improved technique for weapons control, including man-machine interface aspects.
- Development activities on servo systems, involving military vehicle power supplies, trials and analysis.
- Management of software review aspects.
- Chairman of Engineering design reviews.

1986 to 1988

Engineering Manager
Aircraft Systems Ltd, Hawkhurst, Kent

- Group project management of six Sonar Development projects, site and trials work, and studies of various sizes.

Total responsibility for thirty engineers, including personnel related tasks.

– High level contractual and technical customer liaison and internal liaison including marketing, and business management.
– Quality management.
– Member of factory management team.
– Bid Management, including contract responsibility.

1988 to date

Contract Technical Manager
Self-Employed

– Systems Engineering, and consultation of production and product development aspects of photographic studio systems.
– Design of management control and profitability systems.
– Design of financial control and budgeting systems (including management accounting/cash flow control).
– Consultation on production, and pricing strategy.
– Proposal bid and design and development of visual display controller test equipment. Including production and testing.
– Proposal Bids for various design contracts for power supply systems. Including liaison with customers and generation of technical specifications.
– Management of production engineering for the PCB assemblies of a visual display controller system.
– Proposal bid and manufacture of infrared communication system test equipment.

Example 1 – Comments

This is a typical tombstone CV and it can be seen immediately that whilst the information is all there, the potential employer really has to work hard to get at what he or she needs to know to make the important 'must see' decision. Here are just some obvious areas for improvements:

1   There is nothing the employer can buy on the first page. It is all personal details and training, most of which is not relevant to the position being sought.
2   The tombstone layout means that information required by the employer is on the last page.
3   More space is devoted to what was done in the first job 1974 to 1979 than in 1986 to 1988.
4   The job information is all features with little quantification and certainly no benefits.
5   Bald statements such as 'Quality Management' do not mean anything. The employer does not have a crystal ball.
6   Not much thought has been given to the ranking of the responsibilities either in terms of what a potential employer might find exciting or in terms of categories. Engineering and management responsibilities are jumbled up.

Example 2

GREG JONES
15 Buckingham Gardens
Dalston
London E8 IAJ
071-923 3456

Profile

A professionally qualified and highly experienced HUMAN RESOURCES SPECIALIST with extensive knowledge and skills in Training and Development, Recruitment and Selection, Career Counselling, Communications and Employee Relations, gained in a wide range of industrial and commercial sectors. Additionally, has organized and lectured on personnel and industrial management courses, specializing in organizational behaviour.

Key skills

★ Identifying training and development needs and developing appropriate strategies in support of corporate objectives.

★ Designing, developing and implementing training modules and interactive video programmes, with an increasing emphasis on management and sales training, and undertaking post-course validation.

★ Managing substantial human and financial resources, including a department of 25 staff and an annual budget of £1.8 million.

★ Initiating and producing a wide range of training modules, and presenting to all levels of management, up to and including board level.

★ Determining and developing management development and succession planning, through management audit, performance reviews and career counselling.

★ Selecting and recruiting managerial staff across all functions and disciplines, using psychometric testing and Assessment Centre methodology.

★ Lecturing to Polytechnic students and external managers on a wide range of personnel and related business subjects.

Professional qualifications

FELLOW OF THE INSTITUTE OF PERSONNEL
MANAGEMENT (FIPM)
MEMBER OF THE INSTITUTE OF TRAINING
AND DEVELOPMENT (MITD)

Career review – highlights
DALSTON BUILDING SOCIETY   **1980–1992**

Training manager (regions)   **1989–1992**

★ Created new functions to provide dedicated service to branch network sales force in 375 outlets.

★ Recruited and developed training specialists for 12 Regional offices.

★ Designed and introduced a portfolio of business development courses, including customer care, sales and territory planning, cross selling, lead general and sales presentation skills.

★ Developed customized training modules to meet specific local needs.

★ Managed team of 25 specialist and support staff.

Training and development Manager   1988–1989

★ Created and introduced an appraisal system for all levels of staff, linked to a performance related pay system, and fostering an achievement oriented culture.

★ Designed and implemented training courses for assessors, specifically supervisors and above.

★ Initiated interactive video as major training medium and produced IV programmes on a variety of subjects, including a BIVA award-winning programme on 'Assertiveness'.

★ Managed team of 25 training professionals, with a budget in excess of £1 million.

Management training Manager   1985–1988

★ Established training as key strategic activity and as a vehicle for cultural and organizational change.

★ Developed a new approach to management training, employed TA and other techniques, using cost effective overseas venues.

★ Delivered a series of one-week intensive programmes to all management staff, including senior managers and directors.

★ Marketed and sold courses externally to offset internal costs.

Personnel manager   1980–1985

★ Managed and developed a team of 9 personnel professionals and over 62 support staff to cover all personnel activities.

★ Recruited and selected specialist management staff, for all functional areas.

★ Handled and resolved all disciplinary matters referred upwards, sanctioning dismissal where appropriate and managing appeals procedure.

★ Undertook salary surveys, recommended level of annual award and negotiated with Staff Association on Conditions of Service and Benefits.

DALSTON AND LINDFIELD CAREERS SERVICES 1974–1979
Divisional careers officer

★ Managed and developed 11 professional staff in 3 office locations.
★ Determined and implemented annual career counselling and job placement strategy.
★ Liaised with careers teachers and lecturers and provided in-service training.
★ Provided careers counselling and advice to students and their parents.

Previous personnel experience gained in a variety of roles from 1966-73, with HILL SAMUEL, IPC BUSINESS PRESS, NESTLE and MEDICAL RESEARCH COUNCIL. This included employee relations, recruitment and selection and specific project work.

Education and training
LONDON SCHOOL OF ECONOMICS
Postgraduate Diploma in Personnel
Management   1971-1972

SUSSEX COLLEGE FOR THE CAREERS SERVICE
Diploma in Careers Guidance and
Counselling   1973-1974

Personal
Date of Birth: 23 November 1946
Married, one son (15)
and one daughter (12)

Interests
Amateur Dramatics; Cricket; Rugby; Archery; Anglo-
Saxon History; Film Production

Example 2 – Comments
What makes this CV interesting is the Skills summary at the
beginning. What is not immediately apparent is that he is not a
graduate, although you would expect the sorts of jobs he has
done would have such a requirement. This CV shows what can
be done to display your skills in the most acceptable way to a
prospective employer.

Example 3

RICHARD JOHNSON
B.Sc. (Hons), Dip W., MIXX, MIYY

21 Westfield Gardens
Anytown
Herts
AT22 7ZX

0123 123456

Career Summary

A senior marketing professional with significant management experience gained with major US and European high technology multinationals.

An effective thinker and doer offering proven strategic planning, business management and communication skills. Able to work effectively at all levels in organizations with the ability to manage change and achieve commercial profit targets.

Career and Achievements to date:

MARKETING MANAGER,   Jan 91–present
CUSTOMER SERVICE
FASTGROWTH INC, Smalltown

Responsible for marketing hardware and software services portfolio across ten European countries (>£100M revenue). Managed business development, pricing, competitive analysis and new service development to optimize revenue and customer satisfaction. Developed hardware and software business/pricing models matching revenue to channel and distribution costs. Drove specific marketing programmes across Europe. Managed 'end of life' process. A significant part of this role involves the management and successful implementation of change.

SENIOR MARKETING   Sep 89–Jan 91
CONSULTANT
EUROPEAN WHIZZO LTD, Another city
Managed product life cycle and marketing of UNIX/Open Systems and networking in the UK's part of XXX's overall computing strategy. Drove two major product line launches in January and May 90. Was instrumental in increasing market share to 8%. Role involved: pricing; product positioning; formulating competitive strategy for UK marketplace. Produced promotional literature. Presented to major retail and government customers and professional bodies. Ran series of sales training courses on the Open Systems and marketplace for > 100 sales people to prepare them to sell these systems to *The Times* 1000 companies. Marketing responsibility for direct and government sales channels. Drove 'Open Systems' message and management interface with X/Open and the DTI.

PRODUCT MARKETING   Mar 88–Sept 89
MANAGER
LARGE MULTINATIONAL LTD, Greenville
Responsible for development and implementation of marketing strategies for graphics products in UK and Eire and was the primary communications channel between the UK and USA. Conceived and developed new market segments for graphic product – office automaton and process control. Managed OEM and VAR channels for these segments.

SYSTEMS SUPPORT MANAGER   May 85–Mar 88
LARGE MULTINATIONAL LTD, Greenville

Built and managed support business with full P&L responsibility, providing pre- and post-sales support for computer aided design tools for the largest customer base outside the USA. Business was consistently managed within budget meeting both revenue and cost objectives. 1987 revenues – £500K. Success came through effective presentation to senior US management, customers, business partners. Negotiated a £350K system hardware and software upgrade contract. Defined contract terms and conditions and produced sales support material. Successfully set up the UK care users' group. Promoted to Product Marketing Manager.

TECHNICAL SUPPORT   Oct 84- May 85
MANAGER
LARGE MULTINATIONAL LTD, Greenville

Turned round a troubled sales organization in 8 months by setting up a formal software support operation for microprocessor development products running on UNIX and VMS hosts. Raised customer satisfaction levels sufficient to increase and retain repeat sales business from the installed base. Promoted to Systems Support Manager.

SENIOR ENGINEER   Oct 81 – Oct 84
COMPUTER COMPANY, London

Supported PDPI1 and VAX range of processors and VMS, RSX1 I and RSTS/E operating systems. Performed a consultancy role within the support group. Deputized for the group manager to run the day-to-day operations. Additional responsibility for the sale of processor and disk upgrades to the installed base (value £100K) led to an offer of a position as sales executive with target of £1.6M.

ENGINEER   May 80–Oct 81
COMPUTER COMPANY, London

Account responsible for 20 major sites. Achieved consistently high levels of customer satisfaction as measured by customer surveys. Promoted to Senior Engineer.

SYSTEMS ENGINEER   Jul 78–May 80
PROCESS INDUSTRY LTD, Oiltown

Position encompassed all aspects of pre-sales support, customer presentations, project management, in-house acceptance and on-site commissioning of high value process control systems in the Oil, Chemical, Pharmaceutical, Power and Water industries, worldwide. Member of the launch team for XXXX systems. Commissioned the first customer systems.

DESIGN ENGINEER   Jul 76–Jul 78
PROCESS INDUSTRY LTD, Oiltown
Designed analog and digital electronics, microprocessors/ miscrosequenced control systems, telemetry systems and interfaces to PDP1 and PDP8 processors. Promoted to Systems Engineer.

Professional and Personal information
Professional: Diploma in something professional
                      Education establishment 1989
                      Member of Professional Institution XX

Member of Professional Institution YY
Won the xxxxxxxxxx Award for 1990

Qualifications:	B.Sc. (Hons), 2.1 Electronic Engineering	
	Good University	1976
	A Levels –	
	4 Subjects London Board	1973
	GCSEs –	
	11 subjects London Board	1971
Training:	Progressive management training including: Marketing, Product Marketing, Direct Marketing, Professional Selling Skills, Presentation Skills, Finance, Time Management, Project Management, Problem Solving (Advantage & Analytical Trouble Shooting), Team Building Various technical training courses covering hardware, software and networking	
Outside Interests:	Elected Chairman of xxxxxxxxxx Club 1989–1991 Elected Secretary of xxxxxxxxx Club 1988–89 Photography, Bridge, Skiing	
Personal:	Date of Birth: 17.10.55 Status: Married, 1 child Driving Licence: Full UK	

Example 3 – Comments

Despite using prose, rather than bullet points, this CV works well. Some of the better points worth mentioning include:

1   The first page includes the career summary. Personally I am

not too taken with front pages because it makes the CV into at least three pages. However here the candidate has included his career summary so that there is something the employer can buy on the first page.

2   Job Title is given before the employer and before the dates of the jobs held. Just as well really, because this applicant does not stay in jobs for long. By putting dates on the right hand the jobs tenure, or the lack of it, is not so obvious.

3   Job achievements decrease as we are taken back through the employment history, thus reducing unnecessary information yet having the effects of highlighting current skills and achievements.

Example 4

Dominic David Jobs

Résumé

5 Navarino Grove
Dalston
London E8 IAJ
Tel: 071-932 3456

Has strong technical background including Unix, C, Networks and Graphics and good communication and presentation skills, and a deep understanding of the Unix industry, products and markets. Looking for a role that includes significant customer contact, with the opportunity to contribute to produce and corporate strategy.

Career to date

European Graphics Marketing Manager,
Fastgrowth Europe Inc. 3 yrs

Representing Europe's requirements in Corporate, and providing leadership to the country marketing and sales organizations. Activities include customer presentations, major account support, press interviews, non-disclosure presentations etc. Projects include product introductions and transitions, a server market study (with KPMG) and collateral production, and magazine articles. Contributions made in product positioning and corporate strategy presentations. Covered most product areas in addition to graphics.

Pre-Sales Technical Consultant,
Fastgrowth UK Ltd   4.5 yrs

I was the eleventh employee at Fastgrowth UK, the third software person. Initially covered pre- and post-technical support, specializing in Windows, Graphics and Networking. Presented to customers on many technical and strategic areas and gave some of the early customer and internal training classes. Became the presenter of choice in many subject areas. Installed most of Fast-growth UK's internal UNIX systems in the early days. Built the European portion of Fastgrowth's XXX/IP wide area network.

Development Engineer, Help Ltd
(Medical Electronics)   6.5 yrs

System, electronics and software design. Later consulting on all development projects. Designed (still) the best selling EMG (neurological diagnostics equipment). Short stay in marketing to launch the product. Introduced C and Unix as the development environment.

Development Engineer, Kind Devices
(Industrial Electronics)   2 yrs

Electronics and software design. Also sys admin & RPG programming of IBM S/32.

Production Test Engineer, Transecon
(Test and Management)   1 yr

Fault finding and calibration of product units.

Lab Technician, New Band
(Bare PCB manufacture)   9 months

Maintenance of etch and plating chemical processes.

Example 4– Comments

This is an example of an American style CV. Because of the rigorous equality legislation it is not necessary to include much personal information, but this only emphasizes the strength of experience this exceptional candidate offers.

What is good here includes:

1   All the information fits on one page.
2   This candidate in fact has no formal qualification in engineering or computing but has obviously held jobs requiring graduate if not post-graduate status. The education section is omitted but the experience speaks for itself.

Chapter 49 Example Career Statements

How these are constructed is outlined in Chapter 21. Some Careers Advisers and many head hunters, it should be noted, do not approve of Career Statements because they are subjective and represent the applicant's view of themselves. In my experience employers find them useful. This is ambiguous and confusing but, as was stated in the beginning of the book, there are no absolute rules. You, the reader, will have to decide.

Secretarial and administrative

Experienced executive secretary. Able to work independently and make decisions. Proven administration and organization ability, supported by good interpersonal skills. Used to working with executive management at the highest level.

A technically aware sales co-ordinator who has good

communication and organizational skills, able to work at all levels, is committed and can work on her own initiative.

Enthusiastic Customer Service Co-ordinator with proven ability to control multiple marketing projects within given timescales whilst maintaining a high quality of work and achievement of set goals. A confident communicator both internally and externally.

A reliable, conscientious and loyal administrator with good secretarial, accounting and purchasing skills. A skilled negotiator of office equipment and supplies.

Middle and senior management

An experienced bi-lingual (English-German) Industrial Designer with an extensive knowledge of the European xxx industry. Particularly strong aesthetic skills combine with a developed understanding of manufacturing requirements and commercial reality.

A qualified and motivated Health Manager who is an innovator with a proven record of achievement in implementing change successfully, founded on a comprehensive experience within the health sector from nursing to management strategy.

A highly experienced, motivated Management Accountant with comprehensive career within the Retail and Leisure industry, wishing to pursue his career in an environment where his financial and inter-personal skills will make a positive contribution.

A professional geologist with excellent experience in exploration, basin synthesis, together with sub-surface operations supported by a good knowledge of contractor services and offering proven skills in database design and management.

Human resource manager with recently developed business analysis – information systems – ability, seeks a human resource management role with an opportunity to develop general management and information management interests in a healthcare context.

Executive and directors

A self-motivated and achievement orientated Financial Controller/Director with strong business development skills and a proven record of profit improvement through planning and implementing financial and MIS strategies.

An experienced international general manager with an outstanding track record of maximizing start-up opportunities in highly competitive high technology markets through her high energy, creativity, and a capacity for making things happen.

A confident and creative manager with a proven record of achievement in general and technical management with multinational companies.

A natural team leader in a changing environment with a relaxed style to achieving set goals through the development and motivation of people.

A successful General Manager with Sales and Marketing experience, she utilizes a modern, energetic, versatile and customer oriented style. She advocates teamwork, quality and delegation to build winning profitable companies.

The
Perfect
Interview

Contents

Postscripts I to IV   331

Part 8 – Checklists

Introduction

Over the past few years I have helped thousands of people get the job they wanted. For many people a major difficulty is that they are unskilled in presenting themselves. As a result, they do not always get the jobs they should. And the better people are at their jobs, the less frequently they go to interviews – only poor performers get lots of interview practice!

This book shows you how to present yourself and your skills in the best possible way. Research has shown that interviewers make up their minds very early on in the interview, and that personal chemistry between interviewer and interviewee is more powerful in influencing the recruiter's decision than anything the applicant has achieved! These and other research findings can be used to your advantage.

A good start

Getting an interview is really good news for the job hunter. It means you are almost there. Most people approach an interview with trepidation, thinking of all the reasons why they should *not* get the job. We call these 'wooden legs'. Here are some of the more popular wooden legs:

I will not get the job because:

★ I'm too old/young
★ I'm not/too qualified
★ I'm not/too experienced
★ I've spent too much/little time in my present job

Whilst some anxiety is reasonable and healthy, to take all your wooden legs with you to the interview is just plain daft.

THE GOOD NEWS is:

1 You get an interview only if the interviewer thinks you can do the job on offer. Do you know any interviewer who would deliberately waste their time on no-hopers? Of course not. What you have achieved or not and how that relates to the job can be seen from your curriculum vitae. Thus your perceived 'handicaps' have already been accepted as presenting no significant problem.

2 Not every applicant is seen. Most shortlists consist of only five or six people, so you have a one in six chance of being selected. Now you have to work out what it was in your application or CV that made you attractive to the interviewer and plan how to maximise your strong points.

3 Strange as it may seem, research suggests that interviewing is one of the most unreliable management techniques. This

can work to your advantage: you can train yourself to present the best possible picture of yourself and your accomplishments. It is important always to tell the truth in an interview but, with forethought, rehearsal and good preparation you can present what you have to offer in the most positive and attractive way.

4   The majority of managers have not been trained in interviewing skills. This is particularly true of line managers and senior executives. This puts you in an ideal situation to assist your interviewer to gain the information you wish to give about yourself. Once you have read, practised and acted on the suggestions in this book, you will know more about interviewing than most interviewers. You will be able to enjoy an interview with a professional interviewer and assist those who are not very competent.

Will the interviewer mind you being so skilled? No, it will be a pleasant experience for him or her to interview someone who is so well prepared.

5   You are in total control of the information you give about yourself. The interviewer asks the questions, but you decide how to answer them and what information you will release. The professional interviewer is trained to ask open questions, such as

★   Tell me about yourself?
★   What do you enjoy in your job?
★   Why did you leave that company?
★   What brings you here?

All these questions can be answered in a variety of ways

depending on what you choose to say and what information you decided to give.

6   With a little thought and planning you can decide what questions you will be asked. Most interviewers are human – they have doubts and concerns, hopes and fears like everyone else. Look at your application and/or CV through their eyes. Think about their organization and the requirements of the position on offer and then ask yourself 'What questions would I ask?', 'What would my reservations be if I was considering this application for the position and my job depended on it?' (Just think what happens to interviewers who keep hiring the wrong candidate!) Having run through this process you can anticipate the questions and prepare appropriate answers. But remember you must always tell the truth.

No one would run a marathon without training and being sure of the route. As an interviewee, you can train and know the route from your armchair – well, almost!!

In this book there are lots of tips and hints to help you secure the job and/or the promotion you want. An interview, like an examination, is not the fairest or the best way to make judgements about people, but for most managers it is the only method they have. This book will help you to present yourself in the best possible way to help them make the right decision about you.

There are eight major sections:

1: Preparation for the interview
This is to help you prepare for the interview. It will provide you with an understanding of what an interview is from 'the other

side of the desk' and ways of looking at yourself from an interviewer's point of view.

Most interviewers naturally focus on meeting their own needs. This part of the book helps you to recognize the employer's viewpoint and needs.

2: Looking and behaving the part

Interviewers have so little information upon which to make selection decisions that how you look and behave has far more significance than it deserves. This section will help you present yourself in the best possible way.

3: The interview questions – and how to handle them

The main skill of the interviewer is to ask questions. If you cannot answer them appropriately then your chances of success are minimal.

This section will help you understand why different types of questions are asked.

4: The 100 most popular questions asked by interviewers.

These are the most popular questions that interviewers ask. Work through them and you will be ready for any interview.

5: Managing the interview process

It is not what you do that matters, but the way that you do it. This section helps you understand the context of the interview and how best to deliver your answers to the questions.

6: Getting the best deal

There is no point in getting the job and not being rewarded appropriately. This section covers how to negotiate the best deal that your new employer can afford.

7: After the interview

Some more ways of helping yourself get selected even after the interview is over.

8: Postscripts and checklists

Further ideas and lists to help you succeed.

PART ONE Preparation for the interview

The Best Job-Hunt Book in the World

Chapter 1 Preparation

Job offers are won or lost on the thoroughness of the preparations you make for the interview. Before the employer sees you a lot of work has gone into drawing up job targets, job descriptions and person specifications as well as thinking through start rates, reviews and induction arrangements. Some firms, appreciating how costly the wrong appointment can be, will invest significantly in training all those associated with the selection process. You must match this preparation.

Just as you would not run a marathon without a lot of preparation, so the wise applicant will not approach the interview without getting 'interview fit'. Here is how . . .

Chapter 2 **Pre-Conditioning the Interviewer**

It is well established that the expectations of the interviewer about the candidate formed during the pre-interview stage can be self-fulfilling. Interviewers who expect to encounter a strong candidate treat that candidate differently during the interview from the other applicants. The interviewer who expects good answers or positive responses will create opportunities for the candidate to perform well.

Consequently, anything you can do to create the right impression will be valuable. Here are a few ideas:

★ A professional-looking CV emphasizing your achievements
★ A well-written application form which refers to your CV and/or emphasizes your strengths
★ A strong covering letter detailing how closely you match the job specification and your USPs (see page 208)

★ A positive letter confirming the interview arrangements and how much you are looking forward to the meeting

If the interviewer expects you to be good you will sense this favourable attitude and be encouraged to try even harder to present your strengths. So help the interviewer help you – use the pre-conditioning strategy in presenting yourself strongly beforehand so that you are perceived to be the best candidate.

Chapter 3 Banish 'Wooden Legs'

It is surprising how many people prepare themselves to fail the interview. These are the wooden legs I mentioned earlier and here's a reminder of how they work:

★ I'm too old/young
★ I'm too experienced/inexperienced
★ I'm over/under qualified
★ I'm male/female, etc.

What you should remember is that as you have achieved an interview, your interviewer has accepted whatever limitations you put on yourself. Like everyone else, an interviewer's time is expensive. He or she will invest it in you only if you think you can do the job, so do not be too concerned about your wooden leg – whatever it might be, it is not a problem.

PS: I actually worked with a storesperson of some ten years' duration who thought her artificial leg limited her chances of employment. She now works for a major bank in a clerical capacity!

Chapter 4 The First Rule of Being an Interviewee: Don't Answer Questions

This might come as something of a surprise, but it is one of the most powerful pieces of advice given. Interviewers eat the answers they are fed, so as the interviewee, you must not say anything unless you are prepared to speak to it or expand on what you have said.

The best advice I can give is:

Do Not Answer Questions – Respond to Them

In this way you can control the information you release about yourself. In the interview situation, you are 100 per cent in control of what you say. Interviewers can work only on the information you *give* them, so give them the very best information about yourself.

Dr Kissinger once greeted the press corps with the words 'Which of you have questions for my answers!'

He knew what information he wanted to release on that occasion and you would do well to be in the same position at an interview – knowing what information you wish to release about yourself.

Chapter 5 Use a Career Statement

If you know exactly what sort of job you want or you are going for, then develop a career statement about yourself. This should be used as early as possible in the interview.

A career statement has the advantage of creating the right expectations in the mind of the interviewer, preparing him or her for the information that is to come later.

Here are some examples:

★ I am a highly motivated buyer with a proven record of successful negotiating in technical and commercial settings
★ I am a young and determined professional, with experience across the wide range of insurance product knowledge, experienced in both sales and marketing of new business and skilled in man management

The statement should be brief and powerful, highlighting all your employment 'trump cards', including skills from previous jobs which, if left to be gleaned from your career history, would not be given enough prominence in the context of the particular job you applied for.

Work on a career statement can also help answer those open questions which usually occur during the early part of the interview. The question: 'Tell me about yourself' is a gift to the well-prepared statement.

(For more help see Chapter 21 in the CV Book).

Chapter 6 Talk to Yourself

No, not the first sign of madness, but an important part of getting through the interview.

You use different parts of your brain for thinking and talking. Have you ever had that experience of knowing what to say and yet somehow not being able to get it out of your mouth? At any interview, you are bound to feel some anxiety and this will not improve your fluency.

In our society it is not done to be a self-publicist, so all of us are a little out of practice in talking about ourselves, our work and our achievements. Yet the interview is structured specifically for you to do just that. Keep asking yourself those open questions – How, Why, What and Tell me – and answer them to yourself.

Practise talking about yourself out loud – in the bath, whilst driving – others might think you rather strange, but who cares if you are more likely to get the job!

Research suggests that those who are fluent are rated as:

★ More intelligent
★ Having better interpersonal skills
★ Making better managers

So practise, and develop your fluency for talking about your achievements.

Chapter 7 Up Against the Wall

Suppose you were invited to participate in a rather different recruitment procedure. Your prospective employer lines up all the potential candidates and says, 'Each of you has just 30 words to say who you are and depending on how you answer, I will make a choice.' What would your 30 words be?

In fact, it is a very good discipline. Ask yourself: What am I selling/offering this prospective employer? What do I have that they want and need to help make them more successful?

Prepare the '30-word statement' as an exercise and you will find it transforms your interview chances.

The 30-word statement will do at least two things. First, it will make you think about exactly why an employer should hire you. Second, you will have a quality control mechanism for all that you say in the interview because, unless is supports your 30-word statement, it is best left unsaid. Remember, the employer wants you for your contribution to the organization.

All that you say in the interview should amplify your 30-word statement.

Chapter 8 Check the Buzz

This is particularly good advice for those who have been out of work for a time or those who wish to move from one sector of employment to another, from manufacturing to, say, retailing.

Management activity, just like clothing, goes through 'fashions'. Recent 'fashions' have included:

★ Management by Objectives
★ Material Resource Planning
★ Quality Circles
★ Putting People First
★ Zero Based Budgeting
★ The Pursuit of Excellence
★ Total Quality Management
★ Putting the Customer First

It is important for you to check the buzz for your prospective industry or sector. This is easily done by reading the journals for your sector and/or for your profession. Go back six months and skim through the journals so that you pick up current topics of concern and the buzz words and key phrases that are fashionable.

Wherever possible, use your network into your prospective industry so that you can pick up information first hand. One job searcher I know actually rang several firms as a 'researcher' examining the major issues facing the industry that she was interested in entering.

In this way you will be better prepared to answer questions such as:

★ 'What do you know about our industry?'
★ 'As a manager, what issues are of interest to you?'
★ 'What in your view should our organization be doing to improve our position?'
★ 'What do you think we should be doing about the XYZ issue?'
★ 'What major factors do you think are causing us concern right now?'

Chapter 9 Affirmations

Henry Ford said, 'If you think you can or if you think you can't, you're right.'

There is a great lesson here for interviewees because we limit ourselves by our self-image or self-concept.

This is particularly important if you are going for a bigger job with more responsibility but are not absolutely sure that you've got what it takes.

If you are unsure or your confidence level dips during the interview your interviewer will pick it up. Sometimes your attitude is even communicated non-verbally.

A way of overcoming this is to develop affirmations. These are brief statements about yourself in the present tense about what you want to be.

Examples

For a salesman:

'I am an international sales manager with excellent marketing and promotional experience'

For a Human Resources Manager:

'I am a seasoned Human Resources Director with a proven track record of establishing good human resource support and systems in green field situations'

The interesting thing about affirmations is that you actually become what you affirm. This is because you become attracted to and interested in those things which support your affirmation, and you will develop relevant experience and skills. Having affirmations has a direct effect on your environment, yourself and your career.

So in interview terms we can adapt Henry Ford:

'If you think you are, or if you think you are not, you're right'

Chapter 10 Interview Structures

Interviewers are trained, not born! This means that you can have access to the same information.

Interviewers are trained in two major areas: how to ask questions and how to structure an interview. How to respond to the questions they are trained to ask is fully covered later in this book, but here let us examine interview structures.

Interview structures ensure that all significant aspects of the candidate are covered during the interview. For instance, it is no good offering a sales job to someone who cannot drive, a job in London to someone who lives in Newcastle and won't move, or a job in the defence industry to a pacifist.

If you know the structure then it will assist you in your preparation because you can anticipate the question areas. Also, during the interview if certain types of question are asked you will know which structure your interviewer prefers and thus be able to anticipate other areas the interviewer will be interested in. It is like playing contract bridge – you play much better if you and your partner understand not only your own system but also the system of your opponents!

There are two basic interview structures:

★ The Seven Point Plan (by Alec Rodger)
★ The Five Point Plan (by John Munro Fraser)

The seven point plan

This plan suggests that questions should be asked in the following seven areas:

★ *Physical Aspects*. Does this person have the right health, build, physical charisma and impact for the job on offer?
★ *Attainments*. Does this person have the right academic and professional qualifications (or equivalents) for this job?

Does this person have the right experience and track record to be able to do this job? (60 per cent of the interview will be spent in this section.)
★ *General Intelligence*. How intelligent is the person and how is their intelligence used in their work situation?
★ *Special Aptitudes*. Does this person have any special aptitudes (spatial, linguistic, numerical, etc.) that are directly related to the job?
★ *Interests*. How does this person spend their spare time/money and what does it say about their potential skills and motivations at work?
★ *Disposition*. What is this person's personality and what are the implications for the job?
★ *Circumstances*. What effects have this person's

circumstances had on their career to date and how will their present and future circumstances affect their performance in the job?

Sometimes candidates are asked questions which they feel are irrelevant, but if you know the structure you can understand what lies behind the question.

Would you take on a salesman for a highly competitive market if his interests were collecting stamps and breeding guppies?

Would you take on a cleaner whose brother was a professor, whose sister was a consultant brain surgeon and whose father a high court judge?

But many candidates feel that what they do outside work and what members of their family do are no concern of the interviewer.

The five point plan

Here the main categories are:

- ★ *Impact on Others*. What kind of responses does this person's appearance, speech and manner bring out in other people?
- ★ *Qualifications and Experience*. Does this person have the necessary knowledge and skill to undertake the work required?
- ★ *Innate abilities*. How quickly and accurately does this person's mind work, and what are the implications for the job on offer?
- ★ *Motivation*. What kinds of work appeal to the individual and how much effort is he/she prepared to apply to it?

★   *Emotional Adjustments*. How well adjusted is this person to himself, his situation and his colleagues and what are the implications for the job?

Knowing the structure of the interview will help you to understand what the interviewer is looking for and also help him or her recognize it!

As a good preparation exercise, draw up a seven point plan for the particular job you are going for so that you can anticipate probable question areas and how you might deal with them.

The Best Job-Hunt Book in the World

Chapter 11 Assessment Centres

As early as 1949 a researcher named Wagner showed that the interview as an instrument of selection lacked both reliability and validity. His findings have been replicated frequently since then. Amongst the difficulties of the interview were that candidates were not asked the same questions and when they were asked the same question the answers required from the candidate were obvious. In an attempt to overcome this and other difficulties, selectors together with occupational psychologists have developed what are called Assessment Centres.

At Assessment Centres people (usually in groups), have their abilities measured. There are usually four parts to the Assessment, namely:

1   Psychological Questionnaires attempting to measure individual abilities and personal traits

2 Group Activities to examine how individuals respond in group and/or problem-solving situations
3 Social Activities to see how candidates typically conduct themselves usually over a dinner and/or a plant tour – sometimes cynically called 'Trial by Sherry'
4 One-to-one or Panel Interviews by senior line managers

In this way the selectors can gain more and better information about a candidate. Also, candidates are observed in situations which are more like real work settings. However, even Assessment Centres are not perfect and it is possible to improve your performance significantly with a few simple techniques and strategies for Questionnaires and Social Activities.

Psychological questionnaires

It is not advisable to attempt to fake answers to questionnaires for two reasons. Firstly, if the organization is looking for a definite personality type and you massage your response to fit, it is unlikely that you will be successful. Secondly, if you do massage your scores the assessor is likely to pick up the fact that you are not telling the whole truth. In psychological terms this is called motivated distortion, where someone is trying to present a picture which is not a true reflection of him or herself.

Ability tests, however, are different. You cannot make yourself any cleverer than you are but there is a danger of achieving only a low score if you are out of practice. Just as a darts player is good at adding difficult number combinations because of sheer practice, so it is possible to develop IQ skills up to your full potential. Practice will not make you perfect, but it will help you achieve your personal optimum.

'How to' books on IQ are readily available and it is worthwhile working through one or two to get into the swing of solving problems. Just as if the assessment included a crossword, you would be wise to practise – you might not be able to solve *The Times* crossword in ten minutes, but practice would help. So with IQ questionnaires – you might not get into the top five per cent but you will still do better with practice.

Group activities

These usually take the form of a group discussion or problem-solving situation where the group, usually not more than eight candidates, is invited to reach a consensus solution.

The strategy in these situations, which are assessed by trained observers, is to have a good idea of what is being looked for in a candidate. The criteria may, for example, include skills in:

★ Communication
★ Judgement
★ Reasoning
★ Persuasiveness
★ Problem solving

Candidates at an Assessment Centre should think through what likely characteristics are going to be examined by the observers so that when opportunities occur they can demonstrate their abilities.

It is important to make a *contribution* as the observers will otherwise have nothing to comment upon. You can be an active listener and a full participant but unless you contribute you cannot be assessed. Here are some simple strategies:

★ Learn everyone's name in the group and use names as frequently as possible

★ Summarize other people's positions before you give your own ideas or solutions

★ Help the group understand you by giving reasoned arguments before you give your conclusions

★ When appropriate, remind the group of the objective of the discussion or exercise

★ When appropriate, remind the group of the time constraints for the exercise

★ Find common ground whenever you can by highlighting areas of agreement and/or appealing to common values

★ Towards the end of the exercise make summary statements when you can

★ Make notes and take responsibility for being the scribe for the group, particularly when conclusions or solutions are being agreed

Chapter 12 USPs

USP is a sales term meaning Unique Selling Point. The concept behind the USP is that if there is a range of products of a similar type then a USP will ensure that your product is perceived as different, unique and better.

The concept can be used of candidates. If I shortlist, say, six candidates for a job from 100 or so applicants, each of the six will fit the person specification for the job. It is up to you as the applicant to be able to demonstrate your USP for the position on offer.

Pose the question to yourself: 'What have I got that I can offer which makes me special, or different from other candidates? What makes me fit? What are my USPs?'

Have you got special skills or experience which could get you closer to the job specification? Can you develop knowledge of the sector or job requirements?

Remember that the interviewer usually has to make a

choice between candidates on the day; so the USP concept can be turned into a question for the candidate, e.g.:

'Tell me, why should I select you?'

It will be your USPs that help your selection.

Chapter 13 Anticipate Questions

No one is a perfect fit for any job. No one matches the person specifications in every respect. Any interviewer is going to attempt to identify and probe those areas of your background or experience where you are not up to the specification. These are the areas that put you (and your interviewer) at risk.

Before the interview itself you can prepare to be questioned on these problem areas.

Where you are a good fit as far as skills, qualifications or experience are concerned can be quickly examined and it should be easy for you to respond to close questioning on those areas of your background.

However, you know yourself better than the interviewer does and you are best placed to know where you might fall below the standard, so it is important that you practise your answers. Anticipate how you will let the interviewer know that your apparent lack of skill or experience is not a problem, and emphasize the most relevant skill and experience that you *do* have. Remember, the interviewer already thinks you can do the job, otherwise you would not be there, so it is just a case of giving the right assurance.

Chapter 14 The Interview Objective

It is very important to be clear about what the objective of the interview is – it is not always, as you might expect, to get the job.

A useful saying is 'if you don't know where you are going, you will end up somewhere else'. This is true of the interview.

Your objective could be:

★ To get on the shortlist
★ To get to the interview with the line manager
★ To find out if you want the job or to work for the organization

– a whole host of objectives are legitimate.

If you know what your objective is then you will be able to tailor your answers accordingly.

For instance, if your interviewer is from personnel, it will be a waste of time dazzling him or her with your technical ability. Far better to concentrate on your motivation and team orientation and values.

Before planning the interview, identify and write down your objective for the interview, namely:

★   The objective of this interview is . . .
★   So I must slant my answers towards . . .
★   The points I wish to get across to achieve this objective are . . .

Chapter 15 Position Yourself

Some interesting research has suggested which is the best interview position to increase your chances of being selected.

According to the research, to be interviewed first is the worst. Managers do not interview often. Even personnel professionals do not interview all the time. Consequently it takes time to warm up and get up to interviewing speed. This is even more true of board interviews where there are a group of interviewers. It takes time to settle down, discover the right questions, and generally get into the stride of interviewing.

Almost as bad is being interviewed immediately after lunch or being the last person of the day to be seen. After lunch the interviewer is getting back into stride again and is not at his or her best. Interviews usually overrun, so the last interviewee is usually short-changed in terms of time and attention. It may not sound much, but a five minute cut from a 40-minute interview reduces your chances of getting positive information across by

12.5 per cent. If all your fellow interviewees are as good as you, that is very significant.

Sometimes it is not possible to re-schedule your interview time, in which case you have to rely on all the other strategies. However, it is always worthwhile telephoning to see if a change can be effected. The best position is the next to last for the day.

Sometimes candidates are given a choice of times. Choose well.

The Best
Job-Hunt
Book in
the World

Chapter 16 Practise Bragging

It is part of our cultural heritage not to talk about ourselves and certainly not about our achievements. In the interview the selectors will not know how good you are unless you tell them. It is the job of the candidate to ensure that the interviewer's effort is kept to a minimum, so you must overcome this cultural tendency towards self-deprecation.

Exercise in bragging

Make a list of:
★   5 achievements
★   5 skills, or
★   5 things you are good at, or
★   5 things you are proud of at work

Then invite a colleague to strike off, at random, two from your list of five. You then have five minutes to persuade your colleague that the two items should go back on the list.

This exercise will provide excellent experience in talking about yourself at a time when you were achieving or using your skills at work.

At the end of the exercise, your friend can tell you whether or not the item is allowed back on the list. The reasons you are given will be useful feedback.

You might also like to ask your friend if it sounded as if you were bragging. The answer usually given is 'No. You were just talking about what you did.'

Remember – interviewers will not know how good you are unless you tell them.

PART TWO **Looking and behaving the part**

The Best Job-Hunt Book in the World

Chapter 17 Looking the Part

The way we present ourselves and the way we say things have long been known to be significant. Communication is far more than just the words we use. Alfred Adler said: 'If we want to understand a person . . . we have to close our ears. We only have to look. In this way we can see as in a pantomime.' Four centuries earlier, the advice 'not to watch a person's mouth but his fists' was attributed to Martin Luther.

In the selection institution the interviewer is so anxious to assess candidates that the significance of non-verbal messages is increased. Thus, interviewees must try to control the information about themselves which they communicate non-verbally.

In this section we cover the basics of dress and posture.

Chapter 18 Look Good, Be Good

Interviewers have limited information on which to base their final decision, so how you look has a tremendous influence on your success rate. Research strongly suggests that physical attractiveness influences selection, a phenomenon so well known that it is labelled Impression Management.

The older you are, male or female, the more important this becomes.

If you are out of work you have a golden opportunity to get fit and, more importantly, get to your ideal weight. Employers want people who are vigorous and have the stamina for hard work as well as being able to take stress.

From your CV or application form your interviewer will know how old you are, so age is not a major problem (otherwise your selectors would not be seeing you) but how old you *appear* and how fit you are will be significant.

If other things are equal, the job will go to the person who looks the fittest or appears in good health. Healthy people are attractive people so invest in yourself.

Chapter 19 Dress: The Basic Rules

Because the interviewer is usually the first person to see you from the company when you are seeking employment, how you dress is an important part of your impression management strategy. Of course, interviewers are more interested in what you can do and the skills you possess, but attention to one's clothes can and often does tip the balance. People perceived to be attractive and well-groomed generally receive higher ratings than applicants thought to be unattractive or inappropriately dressed. There is even evidence to suggest that more attractive employees achieve greater career success, so good appearance is generally advisable, not just for the interview.

Here are some basic rules for dress:

★ Dress to suit yourself – style and colour – rather than high fashion
★ Be traditional rather than avant-garde

★ Dress as expensively as you can afford
★ Darker colours are more powerful than lighter colours
★ Get a good haircut
★ Buy good shoes and keep them clean
★ If you buy a new outfit practise wearing it before the interview
★ Less rather than more jewellery
★ Dress to the stereotype of the industry or function
★ Co-ordinate your colours

Chapter 20 # What to Wear

Just as there are fashions in clothes, so there are fashions for styles and colours in organizations. In every organization there is an accepted style of dress.

Because the question 'Will this person fit in?' (see page 244) is dominant in the mind of the interviewer, the interviewee's fit with the corporate style tends to take on a considerable significance.

It is easy to get information on corporate style. First, visit the firm about lunchtime a few days before the interview and notice carefully what people are wearing in terms of style, colour and accessories.

The other source of information is the company's Annual Report which these days features an obligatory picture of members of the board.

Just ask yourself what is the predominant colour and style of clothing, colour of tie, length of hair, etc. You don't have to a be a clone to succeed in work but it might help you get through the interview!

Chapter 21 # Pick Up Clues

It is impossible for any human to spend time in one place and not to alter the environment. Just as you create an impression by what you wear, so will an interviewer create an impression by the personal items in his or her office – from family photographs to golf trophies, from pictures to framed certificates. Is the office neat and tidy or cluttered and confused?

Office planners call them micro-environments. What does the office tell you about your interviewer and the organization? Can this information help you become empathetic to the interviewer? Does it mean you might present yourself or your information in a different way?

Chapter 22 The Handshake

There is no real connection between type of handshake and personality, but there is in the mind of many interviewers. There is so little information to go on about a candidate that anything is likely to be picked up and used, particularly at the beginning of the interview when the first impression is being created. So practise shaking hands firmly.

No one is going to give you a job on the basis of a handshake, but a good friendly and firm handshake may just contribute to the overall impression you wish to create.

Chapter 23 Body Language & NVCs

What we say with our bodies is very powerful, and you can increase your likelihood of success by ensuring that you give out positive non-verbal clues.

The major positive NVCs are as follows:

★ A higher smile rate
★ Nodding the head when the interviewer is speaking
★ Leaning forward while listening and when replying
★ A high level of eye contact (see page 236)

all of which deliver a positive message to the interviewer that you are important which, of course, you are.

The result of all this is that you are more likely to be given a favourable rating than a candidate who does none or very few of these things. However, it is important not to overdo things and it would be sensible to practise.

Chapter 24 Are You sitting Comfortably?

Body language is thought to contribute over 60 per cent to the credibility of what people say, so in the interview situation it is very important to get this aspect correct.

Sit as far back in the chair as possible. If you sit on the edge of the chair because you are anxious, as you relax, and professional interviewers are trained in *rapport* skills, you will lean back awkwardly in the chair. Or if you are asked a difficult or challenging question your body sometimes recoils as if you had been physically hit. Questions such as:

★ Why were you made redundant?
★ Why did you not do better?
★ Why did you fail?

and similar challenges are all likely to have this effect.

If you are sitting correctly you can avoid expressing anxiety in this way, and answer the questions easily and positively (see page 250).

Chapter 25 The Chair, Legs and Hand Positions

The chair

Some interview settings are devised as if in preparation for a negotiation, with the chairs of the interviewer and the interviewee directly opposite one another ready for 'eyeball-to-eyeball' confrontation. This is not helpful because before you start you are forced into an unnatural situation: if you watch people who are friends and colleagues they tend to sit more to the side than opposite each other.

In the interview you can create a more relaxed situation by turning the chair 45 degrees when invited to sit down. This takes a little practice but can be done quite easily, and in itself displays great self-confidence: it is the interviewer's chair in the interviewer's room and you have moved it.

Now that the chair is positioned appropriately, you can show how much you like the interviewer by turning your trunk, head and shoulders towards him so that your shoulders are parallel to his. This will make you appear friendly, warm, receptive and empathetic.

The legs

A 'low cross' or the 'athletic position' is appropriate.

High-crossed legs give the impression of defensiveness which is not appropriate. The athletic position is where your dominant leg is brought under your chair and only the toe of your shoe is touching the floor, while your non-dominant leg is firmly planted on the floor, parallel with the direction of the chair, with both the sole and heel of your shoe in contact with the floor.

This is a very powerful position – it makes you look as if you are ready for action.

The 'athletic position' is not the most suitable for women, who should position the legs in a low cross, or, keeping the legs together, just cross the ankles.

The hands

Keep your hands lower than your elbows. Rest them on your thighs or clasp them in a low steeple. A steeple is where the fingers are dovetailed together with the thumb of your non-dominant hand resting on top of your other thumb. (A high steeple is when the hands in the steeple position are brought higher than the elbows – not so powerful.)

The steeple position is useful for those who fidget or who are likely to flap their hands or arms about when they speak. A rough rule in body language is that the less people move their hands and arms, the more powerful they are. This is because they are used to being listened to and they do not have to resort to gesticulation to get their message across. The technical term for this is Low Peripheral Movement (LPM); so when being interviewed, maintain LPM and you will look even more impressive.

The Best Job-Hunt Book in the World

Chapter 26 Look at the Interviewer

It is important for you to look the interviewer in the eye because this will make you appear more confident.

Research carried out in 1978 identified a positive relationship between qualification for a position and eye contact. Those that had good qualifications but made no eye contact were considered to lack self-confidence and thus be less suitable. Would you put someone in a job who appeared to lack confidence? Of course not, so at the interview look the interviewer in the eye.

Why just at interview? Why don't you practise this anyway? It may even help you in your current business and social life.

Some people have difficulty looking at others 'eyeball-to-eyeball', and if you are one of these, then practise looking at the interviewer's ear. If he or she is more than a metre away they will not be able to tell you are not looking at them. Again, this means practice, so start as soon as possible.

PART THREE

The interview questions – and how to handle them

The Best Job-Hunt Book in the World

Chapter 27 The Three Super Questions

The good news is that interviewers ask only three basic questions. All their questions fall into one of three general areas which are the major concerns of the selector:

★   CAN THIS PERSON DO THE JOB?

★   WILL THIS PERSON DO THE JOB?

★   WILL THIS PERSON FIT IN?

Let us examine them one by one.

The Best Job-Hunt Book in the World

Chapter 28 Super Question 1

Can this person do the job?

This question is about experience, track record, achievements – in short what you have done.

At least 60 per cent of a professional interviewer's time with you will be spent on assessing your experience and how suitable you are for the appointment.

Throughout the interview your interviewer will be asking herself: Has this person got the experience and skills we need to make a contribution to the job on offer?

It is up to you to take any question and respond in such a way that you can deliver information about your skills and experience, e.g.:

★ *'What was it like at xyz?'*
   It gave me an opportunity to do abc and efg. One of the many projects I worked on was hij . . .

★ *'What sort of person do you like to work for?'*
   Looking back over my bosses, I enjoyed working with Mrs Smith because with her I was able to do abc, etc.
★ *'What direction do you see your career taking?'*
   Well, I have good experience in abc and skills in efg so I would obviously like to develop them in . . .

The beauty of being asked open questions (see page 192) is that you can use them to get across the information you think most appropriate.

Chapter 29 Super Question 2

This is the second of the basic questions asked by interviewers. When you have answered super question 1 appropriately the selector will know that you have both the ability and the experience to do the job on offer. You can do the job – but will you? So the second super question is:

'Will this person do the job?'

It is obvious that this question is about your dispositional aspects and your approach to work. How hard-working are you? How motivated, committed, loyal, etc. – all the aspects which convince your potential employer that you will do more than just fulfil your contract. This is the selection equivalent of the retail slogan 'Service with a Smile'. It is that additional commitment to personal excellence, which indicates not only that you are able to do something but the positive way that you will do it.

You can choose to answer most questions about your work and career from this perspective. For example.

Q. *What was it like at ABC Co?*

A. It was interesting. Like all jobs the work fluctuated but at ABC you couldn't predict when. So it was necessary to be highly flexible, work within changing parameters and, on more than one occasion, stay late and work at weekends.

As you can see, the question could have been answered in terms of ABC's product, market position, management style, technology, etc., but by choosing to answer in terms of 'Will this person do the job?' you have responded to the question. You have begun to address a major concern of the selector.

In preparation for your interview, decide which aspects of your work to date illustrate that you are committed and motivated – that you give more than most. Once you have prepared these illustrations you will be amazed at how often the interviewer will provide you with questions that furnish an opportunity to address this point.

Chapter 30 Super Question 3

Now you have shown you have the ability and the motivation, there is only one area left to cover, but an important one. If birds of a feather flock together, then executives of corporations clone together, so Super Question 3 is:

'Will this person fit in?'

It really does not matter how good you are; unless you fit the company image you are unlikely to get the job.

Organizations are like individuals in that they have character and value systems. Two companies can make the same product but be completely different in their world view. If values are the concern of the organization, and are represented by the organizational persona, it must follow that the company attracts to itself employees who share those values.

The more senior you are in organization, the more important fitting in becomes. At interview, provided you agree with the value system of your potential employers, it is very important for you to take whatever opportunities they may give you to show how you can fit in.

There are four major areas where the value system operates:

★ How people are managed and power is distributed
★ How jobs get done
★ How people relate to one another and how they are motivated
★ How competition is handled in the market place

By reading company literature, and by active listening to employees, including the nuances of the interviewer, you can pick up clues in these vital areas.

Important Note:

If you find yourself at variance with your potential employer's value system you would do well to consider any job offer very carefully. It is very difficult to be successful in a culture to which you feel an outsider. There is more to career success than just technical competence.

Chapter 31 Reduce Their Risk

Have you thought what happens to interviewers who keep getting it wrong? They become interviewees themselves. In a way, each time an interviewer sees an interviewee he puts his job on the line. The interviewer's own career success is based upon making the right decision about candidates, so you can help him or her by reducing the risk.

The process is essentially an easy one to master. As the interviewee, you ask yourself, 'Why am I being asked this question?'

'What is the area of concern of the interviewer? How can I lower the anxiety that lies behind the question? In short – how can I reduce the risk?'

Your role is to choose the best information you have about yourself and give it.

Just as you select clothes from your wardrobe according to where you are going, with different clothes for work and for holidays, in the same way you select the appropriate topics from the wardrobe of your career.

Each experience should be specially selected to reduce the risk of the interviewer. Ensure that by your selection you not only enhance your career chances but also those of your interviewer.

Chapter 32 The Politician – or Don't Say Anything Until Your Brain is in Gear

Having got this far in the book, you will know that every question the interviewer asks has a purpose and that it is unwise to answer until you know:

★ The reason for the question
★ The most appropriate answer
★ How to reply positively (see page 250)

This may sound a tall order but in fact it is very easy because of the wonderful mechanism between our ears called the brain, which can process at a deep level something like 1,500 concepts a minute and process language at about 600 words a minute. Most people speak at about 100 to 120 words a minute, so there is a lot of spare capacity which you can use to your advantage, especially with difficult questions. Do what the politicians do – say nothing until your brain is in gear. Here is an example:

★ Interviewer: *What is the biggest problem you have had to overcome at work recently?*

(This is a nasty question since, when you talk about a problem, even if it is not one of your own making, because of something called Attribution Theory the interviewer will hold you partly responsible.)

So you have to play the politician and reply:

★ *Interviewee*: Thank you, that is an interesting question because I have had, generally speaking, such a good year. However, if I reflect over the last few months . . . let me see . . . Yes, there was one problem which was useful because I learnt so much from it. The situation was . . .

In the 15 seconds it would take you to say the above, you should have been able to work out:

★ The reason for the question
★ The most appropriate answer
★ How to reply positively

One of the easiest ways to fail in an interview is to give a knee-jerk reaction to a well-placed question. Now you understand the principles of 'the politician' you can work out variations for yourself. A word of warning – don't over-use this little tactic.

★ Interviewer: *How old are you now?*
★ *Interviewee*: That is an interesting question because . . .

It just won't do you any good!

Chapter 33 Stay Above the Line

Research suggests that negative information attracts supplementary questions. Good news tends to be accepted at face value.

Also, negative information is more easily remembered than positive information – perhaps because this type of information is being sought by the interviewer.

The answer is simple: ALWAYS TALK ABOVE THE LINE

Think of your career as a horizontal line. This represents time. On the left put another line at right angles. This is your success line. (See Figure 1)

From 0 to +5 is the level of your success and from 0 to -5 is the level of your missed opportunities. Everyone's career has ups and downs. So here is a career line. (See Figure 2)

No one has a perfect career but as you are talking about yours you can choose to release only the positive information. Always

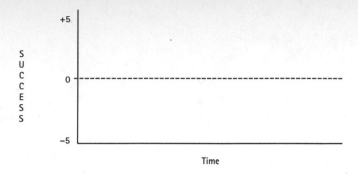

Figure 1

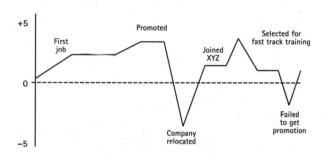

Figure 2

talk 'above' the line. If you are forced below the line then respond to the questions as briefly as possible and lead your interview back above the line.

For example:

★ Question: *But you don't have any recent experience?*
★ *Answer:* Yes, I can appreciate your concern because 'xxxx' skills, I should imagine, are essential to this job. However, I

was promoted to my present job on the strengths of my xxxx experience. Would you like me to outline some examples for you?

How much better this is than, 'No, you're right, I don't have any recent experience.'

Chapter 34 Tell the Story

Interviewers are trained not to ask hypothetical questions of the 'What would you do if?' variety. The reason is that imagined behaviour is significantly different from actual behaviour. Certainly, it would be rare in an interview for someone to volunteer negative information about himself or his skills.

To assist interviewers to deal with reality rather than future fantasy there is a technique called the Patterned Behaviour Description Interview (PBDI). This quite simply asks candidates 'Can you think of a time when you . . . ?' or 'It says on your CV you are . . . Can you talk about an actual example where this was significant?' In terms of real information about a candidate this is far more powerful because you the candidate are talking about real events and what you actually did, not what you think you might/would do.

It is not necessary for you to wait for an interviewer trained in PBDI techniques. Wherever possible tell the story.

Stories are remembered much more readily than adjectives or traits which are applied to individuals. So for a question such as 'How would you describe yourself?' you can reply, 'Fair, creative and hard-working' but where is the evidence? Much better would be a 'When I' story, e.g., 'When I was at Myers I was responsible for all their PR and there was a problem with image so I changed all our publicity material and the result was 24 per cent increase in new clients. So I suppose you could say I was creative and hard-working'. What makes this powerful is that it is a real situation which speaks for itself. Also, the story is more easily remembered.

In your preparation for the interview, work on your real life stories. Do not exaggerate your role or your contribution, but make it as interesting as possible. It was Lord Byron who said, 'The best prophet of the future is the past' so by telling stories of the past you will be telling your prospective employer what you will be doing for them in the future.

Chapter 35 Stress the Benefits

There is an old adage in sales which says 'You sell the sizzle, not the sausage'. In other words, it is the benefit that is bought, not the feature. For example, you might be the best Field Service Engineer there is, but that is not why you are hired. It is because your skills mean minimum downtime. It is the latter which is the real reason for hiring you.

In thinking about your achievements at work, it is always useful to ask yourself the question 'Who benefited from my work and in what way?' Then, when talking about yourself your statements can become what is known as benefit-laden. For example, 'In 199x I exceeded my sales target by 20 per cent (feature) which meant that the company continued to dominate the market (benefit).'

Sometimes it is not easy to identify a benefit. One way is to ask 'So what?' 'So what was the result?' 'So what did this mean?'

'So what could the company now do?' These questions will help you identify the benefit.

It may sound harsh, but employers are far more interested in what you can do for them than in what skills or abilities you have as an individual. The interviewer is trying to establish what benefits you might bring to the organization and where those benefits outweigh those of other candidates.

Present yourself as a benefits package to the interviewer.

It takes a little practice to put together but use phrases such as:

★　. . . which means that . . .
★　. . . which resulted in . . .
★　. . . so that . . .
★　. . . the benefit was . . .
★　. . . we gained because . . .
★　. . . the advantage was . . .

Think of such phrases as hinges which link your feature – a skill or an experience – to the benefit it brought to the employer.

Chapter 36 Explain the Gaps

Customs & Excise officers working in the Green Channel are trained to look for the absence of the ordinary or the presence of the extraordinary because that is what makes people objects of suspicion.

Interviewers are not given the same intense training, but obviously in preparing to interview you they will be using the same sort of principles. What would you have expected in your career in terms of job moves and promotion given your qualifications and experience, and what has actually happened?

Doing exceptionally well will attract as many questions as not coming up to expectations.

'Pushes and Pulls' will be of particular interest. That is to say, what pushed you, or pulled out, out of one job or position and into another.

You must be prepared to talk about these areas because the professional interviewer will probe here for insights into your motivations, aspirations and value systems. Questions about your job will uncover your skills. Questions about the moves you made and why will reveal how you apply your skills and what sort of person you are.

Significant gaps between activities or jobs will attract questions. What was the reason for the year off before university or the six-month gap in your employment record? The wise interviewee will think through suitable answers which can be delivered in a positive manner, e.g.:

★ 'I wanted to travel and broaden my horizons so I planned and self-funded a working tour of North America. It was particularly useful because . . .

★ 'If my career was going to develop in the way that I wanted, it was important for me to review my total situation, undertake a personal SWOT (Strengths, Weaknesses, Opportunities, Threats) analysis and then select the appropriate sector. I had several job offers which I turned down and that is why there was a three-month break. I'm very pleased I did it that way because . . .

Chapter 37 No Tentative Language

Because of a cultural imperative not to push ourselves forward, when we speak about achievement we become self-deprecating and we communicate this in a variety of ways. One of the most damaging is the use of tentative language when talking about hopes and aspirations:

★ I feel I could
★ I think I can
★ Perhaps I would

The use of 'I feel' weakens everything that follows it. There is a world of difference between 'I feel I could do a good job' and 'I could do a good job'.

It is the same with the phrase 'I think'. It dilutes your strengths and abilities.

By avoiding these tentative phrases your statement will

sound far more powerful in the ears of the interviewer. Tentative language encourages a tentative response, but you want to achieve a very definite result.

If you have difficulty making strong 'I' statements about yourself – see the section on 'How to be Humble' (page 261) – and do the bragging exercise a few times with a friend. The interview is one of the few places where it is legitimate to promote yourself and your abilities.

Chapter 38 How to be Humble

Because you are the subject of the interview's interest and, by now anyway, you should be talking as much as possible about your achievements (see page 216), it is difficult not to sound an egoist through the constant use of 'I': I did do this and I did that. Remember that it is more powerful to say 'I did' rather than 'We did', but there are some other strategies that can be employed by using such phrases as:

★ People would say that I . . .
★ Friends have told me that I . . .
★ Colleagues are always saying that I . . .
★ My boss once remarked that I . . .
★ A reference would say that I . . .
★ My experience shows that I . . .
★ The record would show that I . . .

This is rather like getting a third-party reference and is always very useful in presentations to potential buyers. You are not actually blowing your own trumpet but getting the essential information about your achievements across to the interviewer in a more subtle way.

Chapter 39 The Weakness Question

If you get asked questions about your strengths then you will be asked about your weaknesses. This is difficult because you cannot say you do not have any nor can you say you used to be arrogant but now you know you are perfect!

We already know (see page 250) that negative information has a greater significance for interviewers than positive information, so candidates must be very careful indeed as to how they respond to this question.

Remember that you do not have to answer interviewers' questions, only respond to them. The following process approach can be helpful:

1   Choose a trait about your character or personality which is obviously true
2   Extend that trait until it becomes a fault
3   Put it back in the distant past
4   Show how you have overcome it

5   Confirm that it is no longer a problem
6   Stay silent

Here is an example:

★   *'Well, Mr Jones, you have told us all about your strengths. Do you have any weaknesses?'*
★   'Well, I'm the sort of person who likes to get things done and I push myself quite hard. The trouble was, in my first management position, I would push all my subordinates in the same way. Fortunately, I learnt early on that not everyone gives of their best when kept under close supervision, and it was a good lesson to learn.'

Or

★   'I'm the sort of person for whom it is important to get things right, so I'm a great gatherer of information and details. However, I did learn early on in my management career that it is sometimes more important to make the decision than to go on collecting facts. It is a difficult balancing act but I manage my need for detail very well now.'

You can see that by leading with a strength it preconditions the interviewer. In the above example, it is important to get things done or get things right so your weakness will be accepted.

Notice too that the question always comes in the plural: have you any weaknesses? Only ever admit to one and let them specifically ask for another. In my experience, interviewers do not ask candidates for a litany of their sins and omissions. If you do get asked for another, confess to 'working too hard' or 'being over committed'.

Chapter 40 Multiple Questions

You will know if you have an inexperienced interviewer because he or she will fire at you several questions at once.

In such cases, remember that you have been given a choice and you can choose which of the questions you wish to answer. Usually, after your interviewer has asked two or three supplementary questions to your original answer it is likely that he or she will go back to one of the original two or three questions. So exercise your right of choice to your advantage.

However, if you have a professional interviewer (you will recognize this by the constant flow of open questions interspersed with a sudden multiple question), then you use a different tack. There is a school of interviewing which suggests that an answer to a triple question gives an indication of the intelligence of the applicant:

★   Answer one question = average ability

★   Answer two questions = above average
★   Answer three questions = very bright

An example would be:

>   *'How has your job changed in the last three years,*
>   *how have you managed the changes and what are*
>   *the implications for the future?'*

A good strategy here is to hold all the points in your mind by repeating the question.

Chapter 41 The Topical Question

Personnel interviewers are trained to discover what they can about you, not just as an employee but as a person. The two most popular ways of doing this are asking you either about what you do in your free time (see the section on interests on page 269) or what has taken your interest in the news lately.

The theory is that what takes your interest will in some way hint at your values, motivations and in some cases your belief systems. It is difficult to discuss Northern Ireland, world starvation or the greenhouse effect and not reveal something about yourself.

The 'topical' questions can also indicate how rounded a person you are, and whether you are able to see beyond the confines of the world of work.

Now that you know what lies behind the question, you can anticipate it and prepare topics and answers.

For obvious reasons, it is very important for you to give pros and cons on both sides of an argument and/or be able to speak to the issues, principles or viewpoints of the major protagonists. This will not only show that you are an informed person but also that you:

★ See both sides of an argument
★ Are fluent
★ Are balanced
★ Can make a judgement

Most employers would be very pleased to have employees who could display these talents in the performance of their jobs.

Some topics are almost predictable, for example:

★ Oil companies – The Greenhouse effect
★ Pharmaceuticals – Animal rights
★ Local Government – Privatization
★ Retailing – The inflation rate
★ Customs & Excise – The Channel Tunnel

With a little thought you can probably predict three possible topic areas.

Chapter 42 Interests

Someone once said, 'Play is just as hard as work hut we don't get paid for it'. The reason for this is obvious – we enjoy doing it. It is because we enjoy doing something that makes this such a fascinating question area for interviewers. What someone does with his or her disposable time can reveal to the interviewer so much about that person's individual talents, skills and natural motivations. For instance, take two people doing the same job. One in his spare time goes walking, collects stamps and breeds tropical fish. The other plays squash, belongs to a Rotary club and is interested in amateur dramatics. Their approach to the job and style of work is likely to be highly different and, depending on the organization's culture, one is more likely to be suitable than the other.

So whilst at one level what an individual does with spare time is no concern of the employer, at another level it is. The majority of us are not schizoid – we don't change our personalities once we leave work. Those who are high achievers at work are high achievers in their leisure. Those who are social at work will be social in their leisure time.

Thus the wise interviewee will anticipate and prepare for questions about interests. This is particularly important for young candidates and recent graduates because there is not much on the experience side that the interviewer can use to make predictions about job performance.

It is also important not to give the impression, through having so many interests, that your main reason for working is to fund them.

Where possible it is appropriate to show you have interests that indicate you are social, intellectual and achievement-orientated.

Particularly impressive is where an individual has been elected or voted into an honorary position, for it shows peer group acceptance of the individual. It also shows that he or she must have organizational and persuasive skills which are immediately transferable to any management or executive position, and thus useful to a potential employer.

Questions to anticipate are:

★ What do you do in your spare time?
★ Why do you do that?
★ What satisfaction does it give you?
★ How long have you had that interest?
★ What have you achieved through that interest?

There is a danger when you share a common interest with your interviewer that you may burn up valuable time talking about your interests and not the skills and experience which make you suitable for the position on offer. This means that you must become adept at constantly bringing back the conversation to work, or showing how your interests help you at work.

Chapter 43 Have You Any Questions For Us?

This is usually asked at the end of the interview and it is fraught with danger.

Danger 1: Is it a genuine invitation for a question or is the interviewer only being polite? If it is genuine, and only you will be able to tell, then go ahead, but if not just thank the interviewer for his or her time and confirm your continuing interest in the position.

Danger 2: Some research has suggested that applicants are more likely to be rejected if they break out of the role of interviewee and interview the interviewer by asking for information, opinions or suggestions.

The recommended strategy is as follows. Now that you have been interviewed, you should have a clearer idea of what the employers are looking for, so you can hone your 30-word statement to match their needs with your skills and experience (see page 194). You can also take advantage of a sales technique called the 'Assumptive Close'. This assumes that you have the sale – in your case that you have the job on offer. So on being asked 'Have you any questions for us?', your reply can be something along the following lines:

★ Yes. But may I say how much I have enjoyed our discussion (it costs nothing to be polite) and I would like to say now that I am definitely interested in joining you (shows you are motivated) because ....
....
(amended 30-word statement).

Now the question I would like to ask is 'What would be the key result areas of the job in the first six months?' or (being more aggressive):

★ 'What would you expect me to achieve in the first six months after the appointment?' (Assumptive Close)

The advantage of this question is that it gets you off the job description which is usually prepared by personnel and into job targets which is why the job really exists.

An additional advantage is that you can then pull out anything from your experience that you have not had an opportunity to talk about but has a direct bearing on the specified key result areas. You can then say:

'Thank you. That has been very helpful, perhaps then it would be helpful for you to know that in 19xx I . . .' (tell the story of your experience)

What you have successfully done is:

- ★ Not broken role as the interviewee
- ★ Been able to extend the interview
- ★ Got across evidence about yourself that is directly relevant to the real job
- ★ Concluded the interview on a positive note

PART FOUR The 100 most popular questions asked by interviewers

Chapter 44 100 Popular Questions

These are the most popular questions asked by interviewers apart from the appropriate technical questions about your specific skills and experience.

As an exercise it is well worth writing out answers for each question rather than just thinking them through. There is a real difference between knowing what you want to say and being able to deliver a satisfactory answer despite the anxiety of the interview.

Obviously, it cannot be guaranteed that you will be asked any of these questions but if you practise (see page 192), you can go to the interview with the confidence that whatever you are asked you will be able to respond positively.

100 Questions

1 Why do you want this job?

2 Tell me about yourself?

3 Why should we hire you?

4 What is your major achievement?

5 What do you consider yourself good at doing?

6 What sort of person are you?

7 What are your strengths?

8 What are your weaknesses?

9 What do you know about our organization?

10 How would you approach this job?

11 How do you get things done?

12 How do you manage your staff?

13 What do you look for in a manager?

14 What do you look for in a subordinate?

15 How do you decide on your objectives?

16 How do you manage your day?

17 What interests you most in your work?

18 What have you read recently that has taken your interest?

19 What sort of things do you like to delegate?

20 What do you do in your spare time?

21 In what environment do you work best?

22 How did you change the job?

23 What motivates you?

24 If you could change your current job in any way how would you do it?

25 If you could change your organization in any way how would you do it?

26 How have you changed over the last five years?

27 Where do you see yourself going in the next five years?

28 Describe a time when you felt you were doing well.

29 Describe a time when you felt that things were not going too well.
30 How do you work in a team?
31 What contribution do you make to a team?
32 What would your colleagues say about you?
33 How would your boss describe your work?
34 Describe your ideal work environment.
35 Tell me about a time when you successfully managed a difficult situation at work.
36 When were you most happy at work?
37 Describe a difficult situation and what you did about it.
38 Who are you working best with just now? Why?
39 Who are you finding it difficult to work with right now? Why?
40 Describe how you typically approach a project.
41 Given a choice in your work what do you like to do first?
42 On holiday, what do you miss most about your work?
43 Given a choice, what would you leave till last in your work?
44 What do you think you can bring to this position?
45 What do you think you can bring to this company?
46 How do you see this job developing?
47 You seem not to have too much experience in xxxx?
48 We prefer older/younger candidates.
49 You seem over/under qualified for this job.
50 Why did you leave xyz?
51 Why are you dissatisfied with your present job?
52 Why are you considering leaving your present job?
53 Why have you stayed so long/for such a short while with your present company?
54 Why were you out of work so long?
55 Why were you made redundant/let go/fired?
56 If we asked for a reference what would it say about you?

57 What sort of salary are you expecting?

58 What do you think is your market value?

59 On a scale of 1 to 10, with 10 being the highest, how important is your work to you? Why not 10?

60 How did you get your last job?

61 Why were you transferred/promoted?

62 Do you like to work in a team or on your own?

63 What do you like best about your present job?

64 What do you like best about your present organization?

65 What did you learn in that job?

66 What did you learn from the xyz organization's approach?

67 How did that job influence your career?

68 If you did not have to work what would you do? Why?

69 Given the achievements in your CV why is your salary so low/high?

70 What will you do if you don't get this job?

71 What other job have you applied for recently?

72 How could your boss improve his/her management of you?

73 What decisions do you find easy to make?

74 What decisions do you find difficult to make?

75 How does this job fit into your career plan?

76 How long do you plan to stay with this company?

77 From your CV it would seem that you move every so many years. Why is this?

78 When do you plan to retire?

79 What will you do in your retirement?

80 What training courses have you been on?

81 What training have you had for this job?

82 On what do you spend your disposable income?

83 On taking this job, what would be your major contribution?

84 How do you get the best out of people?

85 Which of your jobs have given you the greatest satisfaction?

86 How do you respond under stress? Can you provide a recent example?

87 This job has a large component of travel/sales/negotiation/stress. How will you cope with that?

88 What support/training will you need to do this job?

89 What will you look forward to most in this job?

90 What sort of person are you socially?

91 In your view, what are the major problems/opportunities facing this company/industry/sector?

92 How did you get into this line of work?

93 What other irons do you have in the fire for your next job?

94 What will be your key target in this job if we appoint you?

95 What aspects of this job would you delegate?

96 What makes you think you can be successful with us?

97 What are the major influences that encourage you to take a job?

98 How does the job sound to you?

99 What questions have you for us?

100 Have you been coached in interviewing skills?

Chapter 45 50 Likely Interview Questions for Graduates

Milkround interviews are usually for screening purposes and consequently questions and the areas probed are general. The fact that you will have a degree in the discipline required by the recruiter usually means that the first question 'Can this person do the job?' (see page 240) has been answered. This being so, the thrust of the interview will be in the areas of motivation, personal style and interpersonal skills.

It is obviously not possible to guarantee questions in interviews, but the following pages carry examples from the four major topic areas together with suggestions as to the more popular questions. A good method of preparation would be to write out an answer for each question. If you do this you will discover that there is a significant difference between 'knowing the answer' and 'giving the answer'. It is far better for you to discover this problem before the interview than during it! Writing out the answers will also encourage you to select the most powerful examples and words. It is surprising what nerves can do to one's fluency during the interview itself. Once you have written out your answers it is suggested that you practise them out loud (see page 192) so that your fluency at interview will be at its optimum.

The Question examples that follow have been grouped together into four major categories, but remember that interviewers will not always be as structured.

Questions about your course/degree

1   How did you come to choose your degree/discipline?
2   Why did you come to this college/university?
3   What do you like most/least about your subject?
4   What class of degree do you anticipate gaining? Why?
5   How will your studies relate to your work?
6   How have your studies been funded?
7   Tell me about any project work you have undertaken?
8   What is your strongest/weakest subject? Why?
9   What have you contributed to the university?
10 What have you enjoyed most at university?
11 How does the approach to your subject at this college differ from that of other establishments?
12 What recent developments in your discipline have taken your interest recently?

Career questions

13 Tell me about your career aspirations?
14 Where do you see yourself in 5/10 years' time?
15 What attracted you to this industry/sector?
16 How will your studies support your career? (Note: This is a very likely question if, for example, you are a geographer who wants to be an accountant or a physicist who wants to go into personnel)
17 What are you looking for in a career?
18 Describe your ideal employer.
19 What are you looking for in a job?
20 What plans do you have to gain further qualifications?
21 Why are you interested in management?
22 Tell me something about your ambitions?

Potential employer questions

23 Why did you apply to us?
24 How much do you know about our organization?
25 Do you know anyone who works for us?
26 What aspect of your training are you looking forward to most?
27 Why should we select you?
28 What do you think you have to offer?
29 Where are you prepared to work?
30 What do you suppose are the main problems and opportunities facing our organization/industry/sector at this time?
31 Given your career plans how long will you stay with our organization?

Questions about your personality and interests

32 How would you describe yourself? Can you give me some examples from your life to support your statements?

33 How would your friends describe you?

34 How would your tutor describe you?

35 What are your strengths?

36 What are your weaknesses?

37 What do you look for in a good manager? What sort of manager do you think you will make?

38 What are your interests outside your studies?

39 How do you spend your spare time?

40 How do you spend your vacations?

41 What newspaper do you read? Why?

42 What have you read recently that has taken your interest?

43 On what does most of your disposable income go?

44 How have your interests changed since coming up to university?

45 What motivates you?

46 Tell me about any of your sporting activities?

47 Besides your degree, what else do you feel you have gained from university?

48 In what societies are you active?

49 What positions of responsibility do you hold/have you held?

50 Apart from your studies, what will you remember most about your college days?

Miscellaneous questions

51 Tell me a little about your family.

52 What do your parents think about your chosen career?

53 What will you do if we do not take you?

54 What other firms/organizations have you applied to?

PART FIVE

Managing
the interview
process

The Best
Job-Hunt
Book in
the World

Chapter 46 Interview Start and Finish

Remember that the interview starts when you arrive at the car park or the reception area and finishes when you leave the premises.

So many people lose their interview by their behaviour before and after 'the interview'.

Secretaries and departmental staff are frequently asked their opinions of candidates, so your behaviour here is critical. Some older men have the unfortunate habit of going into 'flirt' mode which does them no favours. Relationships just need to be polite, friendly and formal.

Some interviewers make it a practice to escort candidates to and from reception. This is more than courtesy, for you can tell a lot about a person by what they show an interest in. One major national retailer has what it calls the 'staircase' test. Potential store managers are met in the store by the interviewer who then literally runs up the stairs to the office for the interview. If the candidate can keep up and not lose his breath he has passed the first part of the interview for a job where physical stamina is important!

It is the same at the end of 'the interview'. In my own experience I can remember saying to a particularly nervous candidate after the formal interview, as I was escorting him to reception, 'Well, that wasn't so bad, was it?' Only to get the reply 'No, and thank you for not asking me about . . .' The lesson here is that the interview is never over until you are out of sight and earshot of *all* company personnel.

The Best Job-Hunt Book in the World

Chapter 47 First & Last: Primacy & Recency

The first seven seconds

According to a university study,* people make eleven decisions about us during the first seven seconds of contact. They are:

1. Education Level
2. Economic Level
3. Perceived Credibility, Believability, Competence and Honesty
4. Trustworthiness
5. Level of Sophistication
6. Sex Role Identification
7. Level of Success

*Source: Michael Solomon, PhD, Social Psychologist, Chairman, Marketing Department, Graduate School of Business, N.Y.U)

8   Political Background
9   Religious Background
10 Ethnic Background
11 Social/Professional/Sexual Desirability

That's pretty interesting, isn't it? Just think, all of the above in seven seconds. What is the implication of this when you go for your next interview?

How might you strengthen your first impression?

In 1979 three social scientists wrote a paper which suggested that final judgements can be unduly influenced by initial impressions. Since interviewers are human, they are not immune from the primacy effect. Once an interviewer has formed an impression of you it is often difficult to change that impression.

In popular language, you can only make a first impression once and consequently you must make the most of that very first encounter by

★   The way you dress (see page 224)
★   Your smile rate and eye contact (see page 236)
★   Your body language (see page 230)
★   Early use of your 30-word statement (see page 194)

You can draw a graph of what interviewers remember of an interview against times. You can see below it is shaped like a 'U' because the interviewer remembers the first impression you make and, of course, the last impression you make.

If you plot an interviewee's performance over time you get an inverted 'U' curve because it takes time for you to get into your stride and then you have difficulty maintaining your performance. Your graph during the interview looks like this:

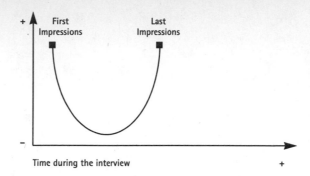

What is remembered by the interviewer

Figure 3 First and last impression

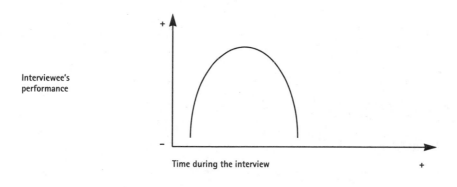

Interviewee's performance

Figure 4 Interview performance

So you can see that when you are at your best, the interviewer is not at his or her most receptive.

In psychological terms what happens is this: once an impression is formed it acts like a filter in the mind of the interviewer. Only information which supports the first impression is allowed through. If information is given which is contrary to the first impression, it is either filtered out or diluted quite considerably.

Take advantage of the Primacy effect (i.e., first impression) and Recency effect (i.e., last or most recent impression) by starting and finishing your interview strongly. You can do this by the use of your 30-word statement (see page 194).

Chapter 48 The Interview: Arrive Early

How early is early? Well, about 30 minutes. There are a whole lot of reasons why you should do this, but here are just some of them:

1   If you plan to arrive early it will give you a time buffer against the unforeseen traffic jam; getting lost; not being able to park. If selectors have arranged to see six or seven candidates on one day and you are late, don't expect your interview to be extended. Your lateness will be interpreted as lack of motivation, planning or self-management.

2   Most people going for career interviews are anxious. It is not possible for the body to stay in high arousal for an extended period and you will find that the longer you stay in your prospective employer's organization, the more you will be able to relax.

3   Arriving early provides you with an opportunity to use the

facilities, so at least you won't have that problem during the interview!

4 It will give you time to read additional information about the prospective employer. Large companies usually have copies of their house journal or product/service brochures on display.

5 Being early will give you time to take in the atmosphere of the place. On your way to the washroom watch and observe how people are working. Open-plan offices reveal a lot about the culture and ethos of an employer: look at notice boards, and read everything you can. You might even see the job you are going to be interviewed for under the internal vacancies section.

6 Finally, the previous candidate may not have shown up and you then have the advantage of an extended interview by being earlier.

Chapter 49 Divest

One of the reasons for arriving early is so that you can divest yourself of everything that is not essential for the interview.

It is only outsiders who walk into offices with their coats or bags. It is only salesmen who go into offices with bulging briefcases. Get rid of as much as you can. What you need in your briefcase for the interview should not be seen by the interviewer and it will include:

★ Clothes brush
★ Hair brush
★ Shoe shine
★ Peppermints

all of which should be used before the interview itself so that you can look your best and can create that all-important first impression.

What do you take in with you? All you need is a clear plastic folder with the following things in it:

★ Company accounts
★ Correspondence about the interview
★ A list of dates when you are free to return for the next stage of the selection
★ Copy of the CV that your interviewer has

On top of the plastic folder you should have a yellow sticker or note paper with the following written in very light pencil

★ Your 30-word statement (page 194)
★ Your USPs (page 208)
★ Company information

Why a plastic file and not a briefcase? Employees walk round with files, outsiders bring briefcases. Why clear plastic? So that the Company Report will be visible and will let the interviewer know that you have done some research on the organization.

Why so little? Because there is less clutter and it is easy for you to sit with grace and leave in the same way.

Receptionists will look after your belongings.

Chapter 50 Watch the Layout

How you are expected to behave as an interviewee is not only suggested by the style of the interviewer but also by the way that the interview room is laid out.

There are three basic layouts used by interviewers.

★ *Across the table*: the classic negotiation style, eyeball-to-eyeball
★ *Across the corner of the table*: the classic colleague style with face-to-face discussions
★ *Across open space*: the classic country club style, friend-to-friend

The range is from formal to informal and is usually a clue to how the interview will be: structured, semi-structured, unstructured.

It also gives an indication of the interviewer's confidence, experience and status. It takes confidence and experience to manage an 'informal' arrangement. The interviewer is relinquishing the trappings of status such as distance (provided by the desk), and comfort (interviewees have less comfortable chairs). It is an indication of status because it is only very senior people who have this type of furniture in their offices.

Since much of our contribution is communicated non-verbally (see page 230) the interviewee is most vulnerable in the informal setting. This is because the interviewee cannot hide behind the other side of the desk. It is well known that feet and leg movements are a far greater indication of confidence than what happens to arms and face. The interviewer has a distinct advantage when your whole body is on show rather than just the top half.

The main point of this section is to suggest that whatever office layout you encounter for the interview, let it affect only your style and not the content of what you say or your delivery.

Even in an informal interview, what you say should still be packed with your achievements (see page 216), and examples (see page 253). It is just that you present them in a more formal way.

Chapter 51 Do not Argue with the Interviewer

There is psychological jargon which is known as the second false assumption of Attribution Theory. Roughly translated it means, 'Interviewers believe that people behave in interviews the same way as they do at work.'

This is obviously not so because both you the candidate and the interviewer are on your best (or politest) behaviour. (The jargon for this phenomenon is Motivated Distortion.) This means that you would be unwise to take on the interviewer head to head, even if you felt it was warranted. Sometimes when you have a good CV which has got you through to the interview, although you do not quite fit the job specification, the interviewer may be quite challenging, and put questions such as: 'Most of your experience would appear mainly to be in . . .' or 'Your qualifications are in physics rather than engineering . . .'

You will do yourself no favours if you remind the

interviewer that this information was on your CV anyway.

This is the process which you can employ to make yourself as attractive as possible without challenging the interviewer:

The Process:

1 Agree with the interviewer
2 Softening statement
3 State your position
4 Show how it relates to the specific need
5 Confirm that it is not a problem

The Example

Your main qualifications are in physics.

1 Yes, that is quite correct.
2 As an engineering manager I can appreciate your querying this particular point; however
3 my physics training has also assisted me in understanding the basic fundamentals of engineering
4 and my x years experience in engineering development have given me a very thorough practical understanding which I have always found more useful in the job of design engineer than the theory alone.
5 So I see a physics qualification as an added advantage to this type of position.

This section relates very closely to the hints on 'Reducing the Interviewer's Risk' (see page 246).

Chapter 52 What Happens Next?

No salesman would think of leaving a prospect unless he was quite clear about the next stage. You must be the same – do not leave the interview until you know what happens next and when it is likely to happen.

You need to know whether there will be a further interview, a medical or psychological tests. You need to know if this is the final stage or if you (and maybe your spouse) will be entertained to see how you get on in a social context.

Without this information you will be left in a sort of candidate limbo not knowing what to do or whether you should be doing anything.

Finding out what happens next will also show that you are not only highly motivated but also well organized, the sort of person who likes to know where he stands and can take the appropriate action.

It may also enable you to get that essential information for the next stage. Who will you be seeing, what is their name and job title, how do they fit into the selection process.

Remember too what was said about positioning yourself (page 214) and use this to get the pole question for the next stage or the offer of employment.

So do not leave the interview without knowing what happens next.

Chapter 53 Don't Eat, Drink, Smoke or Be Merry

You are going to be busy enough working out and answering questions not to mention sitting correctly (see page 231), so don't put yourself into overload by taking on even more tasks.

It would be unnatural if you were not somewhat anxious (high arousal) in an interview and this can sometimes interfere with simple eye-hand coordination (psycho-motor function). At best, you will cope, but when you are drinking coffee you are not able to talk about yourself – at worst, you shake and rattle the cup and saucer. In my experience, about one in 20 people at interview spill their drink in the saucer and about one in 150 actually knock the drink over because of their anxiety. Don't accept the coffee in the first place.

Don't eat either, for the same reason. Biscuits are fine but crumbs get everywhere and, in high anxiety situations, some people's digestive systems actually talk back to the interviewer! Don't smoke. The interviewer might be a non-smoking convert, a health fanatic or have just given up. Even if you are offered a cigarette and none of the taboos apply, don't accept. High arousal does funny things to the respiratory function and coughing your way through your answers is not the best approach.

Don't be merry. Selecting a candidate is a serious business for the interviewer – remember what happens if he keeps getting it wrong. There is a time and place for humour but by and large the interview is not the place nor the time. Take your lead from your interviewer as far as humour is concerned but don't lead with the stories or punch lines. Remember interviewers, like lawyers and accountants, are in a risk-averse profession.

Chapter 54 Staying Silent

Interviewing must be quite a lonely job because many interviewers use the opportunity to talk at length to candidates. If you are fortunate enough to have this happen to you, do not worry; it will count in your favour.

Research has shown that the more the interviewer speaks during the interview, the more highly rated is the candidate! This is because if you are providing a sympathetic ear then you cannot be giving any negative information or contra-indications about yourself. So whilst the interviewer is talking, it can only be positive as far as you are concerned.

There is, however, a significant danger. Being an empathetic listener will only impress the interviewer as to how nice you are as a person, not how good you may be as a potential employee. If you are not careful, at the end of the interview you will be thought of as a nice person but there will not be much to commend you to the job. This is where the 30-

word statement comes yet again to the rescue. You must not leave the interview without the delivery of the 30-word statement. For example:

> *Mr Jones, I have so much enjoyed meeting you and*
> *our discussion. Thank you for telling me all about . . .*
> *May I, before I leave, confirm my interest in the*
> *position because (30-word statement).*

As the interviewer has no negative information about you since you, because of being a listener, have not given any and because he approves of you because you listened, your chances are good. If the only information he has is your 30-word statement and he treats all the other candidates in the same way, then your rating in the selection stakes must be very high indeed.

Chapter 55 Avoid DTBs (Defensive Tactical Behaviours)

Remembering that interviewers eat what you feed them, so avoid mentioning negative information about yourself or your work. It is surprising how many candidates actually lead interviewers into this type of area hoping to be saved the Defensive Tactical Behaviours (DTBs) such as making excuses, offering prepared justifications and/or apologies.

Employ DTBs only when you have to, and that is only under direct questioning. Wherever possible, provide a justification and end it on the most positive note you can. There is a school of philosophy that suggests everything happens for a purpose and that good comes out of difficult situations.

Here is an example first of avoidance and then of 'coat-tailing' positive information on to the negative.

★ *'How is your health?'*
   'It is fine just now. I enjoy good health.'

★ *'Why did you qualify your answer with "just now"?'* 'Well, last year I had an ulcer. I was off work for a little while but I soon recovered. It was during that time I decided to do my Open University degree and I started this January.'

In this example, the interviewer will hopefully follow up on the Open University rather than the possibility of a recurring health problem.

The use of DTBs is likely to maintain one's self-esteem because they justify personal inadequacy, but they do not really enhance one's employment opportunities.

Chapter 56 **References**

It is surprising how many people put references on their CV. with the assumption that one person can recommend you for any job for which you can apply.

Even worse is the referee who is chosen for his or her status rather than anything else. Commissioners of Police are useful if you apply to be a policeman or bishops if you wish to be ordained, but by and large the prospective employer is most interested in what you can do in the job. This means that the best reference comes from someone who holds an executive position in the industry or field you wish to join. A reference from a PR director for someone who wants to go into PR will cut far more ice than a local mayor or councillor.

You will not know which referee to give until you have been interviewed, because you will not know what they are looking for until you have been interviewed. The interview will tell you as much about the requirements of the job as it tells your prospective employer about you. Once you have been interviewed you will be in the best position to brief your referees as to what the prospective employer is looking for.

Here is the plan of action:

1 By networking, identify good potential referees in the functional area you wish to join
2 Gain their agreement to act as referees
3 Brief your referees as to your strong points and USPs
4 Give your referees a copy of the CV(s) that you are sending out
5 As late as possible in the selection process select and give the most appropriate referees
6 Contact the referee by phone and tell him or her about

★ The job, company and recruiter
★ The major responsibilities
★ The key targets for the first six months
★ Your USPs for this particular position
★ Ask for copies of references sent

IMPORTANT NOTE: Public sector firms usually require references before the interview; in which case it is best to advise your referees as much about the job as possible. Usually in the public sector full job description and person specifications are available beforehand, so copies of these can be sent as well.

PART SIX

Getting the best deal: negotiating pay and conditions

The Best Job-Hunt Book in the World

Chapter 57 Getting a better deal

The major reason why people move jobs is to ensure that they get a better deal for themselves. Once you have been offered the job all your preparation would be wasted if you were unable to secure an improvement in your financial position.

This section is dedicated to assisting you in getting the best deal you can for yourself.

There is an old adage that if you don't ask, you don't get. This section shows you how. Remember that employers expect you at the end of the selection process to negotiate for yourself. The iron rule of wages says that employers will pay you as little as they can to get, keep and motivate you. It is up to you to help your employer recognize your value and the contribution you can make to the organization.

The Best Job-Hunt Book in the World

Chapter 58 Pay and Conditions (The Basics)

The basic fundamentals of negotiation also apply to discussions on pay. The principles are:

★ Negotiate only from power
★ Negotiate only with decision makers
★ Work to what they can afford, not what you need.

Negotiate only from power

When you are one of one hundred candidates you have no power, but it is surprising how many candidates at CV or covering letter stage state how much they are looking for. Often they are rejected for wanting too much, but the successful candidate may end up being offered more than he or she asked for in the first place.

Nor do you have the power at the first interview because being on the shortlist, you are still one of five or six. The golden rule is leave money matters as late as possible. When you are the final candidate, and it would cost the company a great deal to start up the process again, then you have real power. This is the time to ask for that extra ten per cent or that special fringe benefit.

Negotiate only with decision makers

In selection terms this usually means the senior line manager and not the personnel recruiter. In most cases, the personnel recruiter can only say no; he cannot say yes without going back for approval so, whenever you can, delay discussions on conditions as late as possible.

Work to what they can afford

In large firms and for junior positions there are usually set bands for both pay and benefits but everywhere else they are negotiable, especially at executive level. Usually the '*c*' circa that appears in adverts means ten per cent on either side of the salary quoted. These days it is so expensive to recruit staff that, at executive level, an extra few thousand is far cheaper than starting up the whole recruitment process again. However, to get the company to move you must not only delay discussions on pay as late as possible but also be prepared to negotiate.

Chapter 59 Pay Negotiation Strategies

Basically there are two main negotiation strategies to apply when negotiating your new contract – the Monkey and the Brooklyn Optician.

The monkey

The monkey is the problem or the difficulty and, as the applicant, it is your job to ensure that the monkey is, as far as possible, with the interviewer. Here is a little demonstration of how a pay discussion might go:

★ *Tell me, how much are you looking for?*
(You have the monkey)
★ Well, I know you are a progressive company with a

reputation for looking after your people, so I'm sure you will be paying at the market rate.

(He has the monkey)

★ *Yes, but we have to start somewhere, so what are you expecting?*
(You have the monkey)

★ I might be tempted to overprice myself so perhaps you could tell me what the range is for this appointment. (He has the monkey)

★ *Well, the range is between £x,000 and £y,000 for this position.*
(You have the monkey)

★ I see. Given that I have 'n' years experience and qualified in 'm' how high up the range would you be thinking of offering someone like myself?
(He has the monkey)

★ *We were thinking in the region of £x,000 + 2,000 to start.*
(You have the monkey)

★ [At this point you just stay quiet.
(He has the monkey)

★ *But in your case we could offer £x,000 + 2,000 + N*
(You have the monkey)

★ Thank you. When is your first pay review?
(He has the monkey)

★ *It is in January.*

★ Would it be possible to do something then subject, of course, to my satisfactory performance?
(He has the monkey)

★ *Well, we could let you have the full cost of living component.*
[This has been budgeted anyway]
(You have the monkey: You can either accept or go for more depending on how you judge the situation. If you decide on the latter, then say:)

★ I really would like to join you because ... However, I was expecting a larger salary.

(He has the monkey. However, you are now sailing very close to the wind.)

The dance goes on until you agree a start rate.

The Brooklyn Optician

This optician sells glasses in the following way. In the right-hand column you can see how the price escalates.

The lenses in these glasses are very reasonable.	
They cost only $40 (pause)	$40
each	$80
You can have the standard glasses but this	
particular frame costs $120	$200
If you want it in gold it costs $50 but real	$250
rolled gold is $150	
If you require the glasses within four weeks	
rather than the normal waiting period of six	
months there is a small service charge of $50	$400
etc., etc.	

So what was quite cheap slowly becomes more expensive as the buyer is slowly taken up the price escalator.

The same can be done with fringe benefits. The lines show how the Brooklyn Optician method works:

★ I presume you give medical insurance/at the London

Teaching Hospital rate/for my family
★   I understand it is an executive car/not less than three
    litres/fully expensed/renewable every year
★   I understand there is a mortgage scheme at five per cent
    below base/You pick up the tax element/Can be used as a
    loan facility, etc.

Remember Rule Three – if you do not ask you will not get.

PART SEVEN

After the interview

Chapter 60 Interview, Review and Learn

Every interview is a learning opportunity. However thoroughly you prepare, you can always improve. Treat each interview as a learning opportunity. Did you get the questions you expected? Did you answer the questions as well as you might? Did you help the interviewer as much as you could have done?

You should review your interview performance as soon as possible after the event so that you can learn from the opportunities it provided. Even if you get a PTD (Polite Turn Down), looking at the interview as a learning opportunity will help you get over the disappointment of not being offered the position.

If you do get a PTD it is always useful to call the interviewer and get feedback on where you were strong and where you did not match the specifications. Don't embarrass the interviewer by asking why you didn't get the job. Just ask for feedback on your interview. If you ask for feedback you must listen to it and not try to enter into a debate with your interviewer. Like all feedback, review it and where appropriate make the necessary changes.

Each interview that receives a PTD just brings you that much closer to being successful. You cannot fail at an interview because each interview provides an opportunity to improve and do better next time.

Chapter 61 It Helps to Stay in Touch

In spite of the title of this book, you can always improve on your interview performance. Immediately after the interview you should go through all the questions you were asked and review all your answers. There is always something that you could have/should have said about a skill or experience that you have. However, all is not lost, because you can stay in touch.

Three working days after the interview (usually too soon for you to have been turned down), write to the interviewer as follows:

★   State how much you enjoyed the interview
★   Confirm your continued interest
★   Offer additional information about yourself which will help them in making their decision

This sort of letter works at various levels. First, it gives additional information about yourself directly related to the job requirements. This may be just enough additional information to tip the balance in your favour if you are in close contention with another.

Secondly, like advertising, it keeps your name in front of the buyer, namely the potential employer. You may have not been that memorable out of the six candidates who were seen on that day, but certainly you will be remembered from your letter. It will bring your correspondence and details to the top of the candidate file.

Thirdly, it shows motivation, commitment and loyalty to your prospective employer. If their first choice turns them down, who do you think their second choice would be? Obviously, the person who is keen to join the organization.

You can also use this mechanism for giving an additional referee (see page 311) who can speak directly of a relevant and specific aspect of your experience or skill which was emphasized during the interview.

This mechanism makes you appear keen and 'user friendly' and that in a job is sometimes more important than ability.

So keep in touch.

Chapter 62 Interview Yourself

The first hundred days in any new job are critical to your success in the organization. Most people in new jobs will repeat, in terms of style, approaches and behaviour, those aspects which were successful in their old organization. There is nothing wrong in this for it is sensible to repeat successful behaviour. However, success in one organization does not always transfer into another because of the possibility of differing styles, objectives or culture within each ambiance.

Thus the advice is for you to 'interview yourself' regularly in the new job, asking questions of yourself such as:

★ I know what they said they wanted me to do, but what do they really want?

★ How are people recognized in this organization and what do I have to do to get recognition?

★ Who is thought to be the ideal 'corporate person' in this

organization, what are they like, how am I different from them and do I want to do anything about it?

★ What is my next career move in this organization and what should I be doing now to achieve it?

Postscript I

Now you have got through the book you should be much better prepared for the interview. In the job search stakes you will, when you apply the techniques and strategies, find yourself with multiple job offers.

Your problem, now that employers want you, is to be very clear about what you want from the job and whether a particular offer will satisfy your specific needs. Here are some questions:

★ Will the job meet my immediate and long-term financial needs?
★ Can I or will I be able to do the job on offer satisfactorily?
★ Will I be happy in this position?
★ Will I get on with –
   My boss?
   My subordinates?
   My colleagues?

★ Do I share the values and the mission of the organization?
★ Will I be able to develop my career from this position?
★ Will accepting this job help or hinder my long-term career ambitions?
★ Is the organization part of a growing sector in the economy?

In making the decision about taking a job it is important to remember the formula: 7.5 x 232 x 42.

That is, the hours of work by the number of working days in a year by the number of years you spend at work. To put this into perspective, if you walked at four miles per hour for each hour of work in your lifetime you could cross the Atlantic 18 times. You spend a long time at work. Don't accept a job just because you got through the interview and someone offered it to you.

It is easy to pass the interview; the trick is to make a success of your career.

Postscript II

A question often asked both by individuals I work with and organization clients is about the morality of helping individuals through the interview. Is it right for the individual who is better groomed to get the job than the person who is best qualified?

The difficulty here is to define who is the best candidate. Capitalism in some ways is not unlike evolution: the better prepared the animal is for the environment it will encounter, the more chances it has of survival. The same with candidates in the job race.

My own view is that in a free society people can choose to do the best they can or just muddle along – it is up to them. If people choose to do the best they can at interview I would interpret this positively in terms of commitment, persistence and motivation. Most success at work is about perspiration rather than inspiration. Much of the information in this book is either common sense written large or publicly available in many books, and reading is not a prohibited activity. People can choose to take advantage of what is available to them, or bear the consequences of ignorance.

Postscript III

Another question I'm frequently asked is 'Won't the interviewer know that I have prepared and groomed myself for the interview? The answer to this is no. First, if you have read this book you will know more about interviewing than 90 per cent of managers, who will not have been trained in selection techniques.

Second, if you come up against a professional interviewer both you and he or she will enjoy the process. Try playing squash with someone who is unfit and does not know the rules. It is not much fun. Ask a buyer whom he prefers to work with – a trainee salesman or a professional. Ask a negotiator whom he prefers to negotiate with – a rookie or someone with scar tissue. Most professional people appreciate professionalism in another. Having read this book you will find yourself disappointed at the number of unprofessional interviews you will experience. You will enjoy meeting a professional.

The Best Job-Hunt Book in the World

Postscript IV

This is the most important of all the postscripts. The overriding cardinal rule is:

DO NOT LIE AT INTERVIEW

The whole basis of the interview is that both parties tell the truth. How would you feel if on joining a new organization you were not provided with the salary you were promised, the resources you were led to expect or the subordinates you thought were going to report to you?

You must tell the truth. But in interviewing you can be selective (please see John 18 verse 38). If you have suffered a recent mental illness and you are not asked about your health, there is no need to mention it. If you have been fired for incompetence and you are not asked why you left then there is no need to mention it. I don't know of any product, apart from cigarettes, that comes with a list of its drawbacks or inadequacies freely available at the point of sale. In my view lies of omission are permissible if they are no longer relevant to your likely job candidature or ability. There is an obligation on the part of the interviewer to be skilled enough to ask direct questions if he or she has any doubts about your ability or background.

The Best Job-Hunt Book in the World

Checklist A Pre-Interview Planning

1 What do I know about the company?
  - ★
  - ★
  - ★
  - ★
  - ★

2 What do I know about the job?
  - ★
  - ★
  - ★
  - ★
  - ★

3 What do I know about the interviewer and the selection process?

★

★

★

★

★

4 What is my 30-word response to 'Tell me about yourself?' (see page 194)

★

5 What points are unique about me and support my application? (see page 208)

★

★

★

★

6 What achievements will the interviewer(s) be most interested in?

★

★

★

★

★

7 What possible problem areas are there in my application and how can I put them positively?

★

★

★
★
★

8 What possible question areas will I have for my interviewer(s)?

★
★
★
★
★

9 Who would be my most appropriate referees for this position and what would I like them to say about my experience and achievements?

★
★
★

10 What lasting impression do I want to leave with my interviewer(s)?

★
★
★
★
★

Checklist B The Interview Checklist

Paperwork needed for the interview

- ★ Advert
- ★ CV
- ★ Letter of Application
- ★ Letter of Invitation
- ★ Company Literature
- ★ Plastic folder
- ★ Pre-Interview Planning
- ★ Examples of work
- ★ Photograph

Briefcase contents

★ Hairbrush
★ Clothes brush
★ Toothbrush
★ Nailbrush
★ Shoe brush
★ Peppermints/breath freshener
★ Appropriate newspaper

Note: Remember to get rid of your briefcase with the receptionist (see page 297)

The
Perfect
Career

Contents

Section titles

Strategy

Chapter 1 Strategy

1. Stay mainstream 1

In pursuing your Perfect Career stay wherever you can in the mainstream. I am sure that the great restaurants in Paris have computer specialists working in them and that computer companies in California have chefs working for them. Now it is not impossible but highly unlikely that you will be a world famous chef working for Sun Microsystems or a leading edge computer specialist at George V, Paris, but I'm sure the point is obvious.

A manufacturing specialist is unlikely to be valued highly in a marketing driven firm or vice versa. Whatever your specialism, work in an organization where what you do is mainstream.

Find out which firms have the best reputation for your particular function or the area you wish to specialize in and then do your best to join them. Not only do you get the best training and the best experience, your career will benefit from their reputation.

2. Goals and targets

'Those who don't have personal goals will always be working for those who do.'
  Max A Eggert

At a famous Business School on the first day of their studies students were asked which of them had written down quantifiable personal career goals. Surprisingly, for it was an ivy-league post-graduate school with a global reputation of producing the best, only three per cent of hands went up. Ten years later those three per cent were worth more in financial terms than all the other 97 per cent put together. Now whilst money is not everything, by and large it is not a bad indicator. The career message is clear.

Goals and targets turn dreams and visions of the future into reality. It is trite but right that if you don't know where you are going, anywhere will do. Goals and targets not only give you direction but help you to see the opportunities that others miss. Feeling hungry and driving through a new town you will be far more aware of food shops and restaurants. We look for what we want. If we only have vague ideas of what we want, we will not look for it and then opportunities will not be grasped as they occur.

Capitalism is a great system but it is also dangerous because if you do not have your own personal career objectives you will find yourself working to organizational objectives set down by others. Those who do not find this out early in life will never have a Perfect Career and unfortunately there are many who find out too late.

In most cases people think about their career objectives when they are about to finish their full time education and usually they are highly influenced by family or by school teachers who unfortunately do not always know as much as they should about the world of work or, most of all, about what is available in the local community. Often individuals just drift into any first job without seriously thinking through or being concerned about what sort of career may develop from their choice. Children often follow their parents and this is especially true of the professions.

In my days as a university recruiter I was always mildly surprised to discover that graduates frequently made their first job decisions based upon how much they liked the interviewers on the 'milk round' rather than on where a job in that firm would lead them. This is one of the main reasons why graduates do not stay with their first employer for very long. Many waste the first two years of their career sorting themselves out and in a career spanning 40 years that is a five per cent loss.

The other time when serious thought is allotted to personal career management is, unfortunately, when individuals lose their jobs through redundancy. This is a massive blow to the ego and it certainly makes people think about where their careers are going and who they are working for. Sometimes it takes redundancy for people to realize the hard lesson that the only person who is responsible for their security and their career is themselves.

Goals and targets need to be written down otherwise they stay as dreams and visions. Once goals are written down they take on a reality of their own and you begin to take them seriously. It is strange how at work we have all these skills and expertise (what project is ever submitted for approval without spelling out the objective?), but then do not apply such skills to our personal career situation. At work projects are always being defined and quantified so that they can be appraised. Even on an average manual salary in a lifetime you are likely to earn something approaching £750,000 at today's prices. The fact that you have invested in this book indicates that you will probably hope to earn far more. Now with a £750,000 project or investment don't you think it deserves some serious work on objectives, options and success criteria?

Objectives should be specific. It is not helpful to say 'I want to be famous' or 'I want to be rich' or 'I want to be great'. Everyone dreams this or something like it. Famous at what? Recognized by whom? Honoured in what way? It is not sufficient to be a 'Wannabe'. The more specific you are the more likely you are to be able to achieve the goal. Being specific forces your goals and targets to be less fanciful and more factual; they become more tied to reality; they become more obtainable and achievable.

Once the targets have been written down then it is possible to move on to the next stage which is giving them time frames. This then facilitates a timetable about what has to be done in terms of qualifications, experience and profile. Just like a management project, once the time objectives have been worked out then specific work schedules and resources can be allocated. You will have a programme for the year, the month, the week and even the day if necessary.

Some people have suggested that this takes all the fun and spontaneity out of life, that one becomes dominated by an impersonal system. This is simply not true. Targets just give you a focus but they can always be changed as your values or visions mature. What it does mean, however, is that with goals and targets which are specific and timebound, you will have far more control, far more options and thus far more freedom to do what you want to do with your life.

Alice:	Please sir, can you tell me the way?
Cheshire Cat:	Where are you going?
Alice:	I don't know.
Cheshire Cat:	Then any road will take you there.
	Alice in Wonderland – Lewis Carroll

3. One shot

'To me old age is always 15 years older than 1am.'
   Bernard Baruch

There is no such thing as reincarnation in a career life, although I have met some chief executives who deserve to come back in the humblest capacity possible. In reality, if you don't get your career right first time you don't get sent back to 'Go' to start again and you certainly don't get £200.

Like it or not, we live in an ageist world with a golden decade of thirty – forty for men and, because this world is also sexist, for women it is twenty-five to thirty-five. This means that from the very outset of your career, you have a series of time windows which all begin to close slowly the moment you take your first job. If you aspire to a top position then you have to move as quickly as possible through the ranks otherwise you find that a window is closed blocking future opportunities. You only have to look at the job adverts in quality papers to see the number of age bands there are. Plot your career in job terms and then find similar jobs in the adverts and you can work out 'what you have to do by when' to get to where you want to go.

4. Make mistakes early

'If I had to live my life again, I'd make the same mistakes, only sooner.'
   Tallulah Bankhead

We get things right by getting them wrong. In career terms you cannot make a mistake, you can only give yourself a 'learning opportunity'.

However, it is best to make all your career mistakes earlier rather than later. As your career develops and you move up the corporate ladder, recovery time is extended. Your career is like your body in that the older you are, the longer it takes for bruises to heal and bones to mend.

Most successful people make one major career error but they do it early and they learn from it.

5. Stay mainstream 2

Stay as long as you can in mainstream companies which are in the *Times* Top 100 or Fortune 500. These firms have the reputation and the career equivalent of street credibility. They are the Eton and Harrow of work, the Oxford and Cambridge of careers.

Once you move out from the mainstream into a lesser tributary, your chances of getting back into the swim are minimal. There is always a best and it is worthwhile shooting for it. If you are going to take your career seriously it is worthwhile shooting for the gold bullseye on the target. There is no guarantee that you will get the centre every time but your score rate will be that much higher than if you just aim loosely in the direction of the target, hoping for success.

Because you are successful (and you must be since you have had blue chip experience) you will be very attractive to smaller firms. Take heed, though, this is very much a one way ticket. Once you have left the first division it is difficult to get back. If you have left a blue chip firm for a second division one the reverse trip is difficult as any footballer will tell you.

'Experience is the child of thought, and thought is the child of action.'
Benjamin Disraeli

6. Deal with what you can touch
'All experience is an arch, to build upon.'
Henry Adams

At one time I helped run a small electronics firm at a time when the Pound was getting weaker against the Dollar all the time. Since the firm was American this caused great concern because no matter how efficient the plant was, how hard we worked, how good we were, there was no way that we were going to make the product levels expected of us when our sterling profits were consolidated into dollars.

For a long time we had meeting after meeting to discuss what we could do about the situation until it suddenly dawned on me that there was nothing I could do, nor could the team, nor could anyone – if the Pound dropped through the floor all that we could do was run the most efficient factory possible. No amount of discussion concerning the currency was going to change the situation. In fact, such discussions were a waste of good management time. All we could do was manage what we could touch and that meant having the best production facility run by the best people we could get.

It was an important lesson. I understand that great tennis players don't worry about winning Wimbledon, winning the match, the set or even the game – when under pressure they just concentrate on getting the ball over the net successfully. Just keep doing the best you can with what you have got and you will be successful – not just in the short term but in the long term as well.

When we think about our career we worry a lot about what we should have done or what has happened or, alternatively, we worry about the future and what might happen. All of these are inappropriate behaviours. The past helps you learn from your mistakes and the thinking about the future provides opportunities to anticipate difficulties, but that is all. What you need to do is concentrate on the most important work you should be doing today.

'Jumping at several small opportunities may get us there more quickly than waiting for one big one to come along.'
Hugh Allen

7. Two types of pay
'There is no security in this life. There is only opportunity.'
Douglas MacArthur

Rewards in organizations come in two forms, one obvious in the form of pay and the other more subtle – namely, experience. Both are valuable in their own way but pay in the form of experience is accumulative and, what's more, it is difficult to lose once you have gained it. You can't have an overdraft of experience.

It is usually thought that qualifications are the key for success but this is not so. Only about 15 per cent of managers and executives are qualified for what they do; the other 85 per cent have experience. Qualifications are, of course, important but they only determine how high up the ladder you start (and no one starts at the top!) but it is experience that takes you most of the way in your career. I train hundreds of people every year in how to be interviewed. Not one of them has ever come back from an interview and said they were asked about what class of degree they got, but they all report being asked lots of questions about their experience.

The message is clear – treat experience as seriously as you do your salary. It is strange that employees ask for pay rises and work hard to achieve a bonus but so few ask for the sort of experience they need for their career.

Sometimes employees almost make the ultimate career sacrifice. They stay locked into a boring, dead-end job for years because of the money and all the time their real value in career terms, that is their experience, is continually being devalued.

Take your experience seriously, work hard for it, negotiate for it because it is a key to your perfect career.

'A wise man will make more opportunities than he finds.'
Francis Bacon

8. What's next?

I'm always interested in how people got the jobs they do and am frequently amazed when in answer to the question 'How did you do it?' they just say 'I was offered it.'!! It is as if people are in career drift, in that they accept jobs on the basis that they are offered to them.

Would you start travelling in a certain direction unless it took you where you wanted to go? Would you go into a shop which did not offer what you wanted to buy? Of course not – but it is surprising that people are so flattered to be offered a position that they take it without thinking 'where does it lead – what's next?' Five years down the track they discover themselves sidelined into jobs they do not like or enjoy and which are very difficult to move out of. There is a lovely story about two men travelling down the motorway and one says to the other, 'Where are we going?', only to get the reply 'I don't know, but we're making great time!'

Most employers are not going to give you jobs for the sake of your career development but really to meet pressing and urgent organizational requirements. The first allegiance of the organization is to its owners, then to its customers, next its product or service and finally to its employees. Make sure that you work to fulfil your own objectives rather than those of others. It is legitimate to work for yourself.

'I am not in Wall Street for my health.'
   J P Morgan

9. Pick your boss

Your boss is key to your future so make sure whenever you can that you have a good one, not only in the sense that you will be managed well but also that his or her standing in the organization matches your career aspirations.

You might be brilliant but if your boss is naff then your brilliance will be considerably dulled.

If you can get someone who is a rising star, then,

★   you will learn and develop more quickly
★   when they are promoted you have a good chance of getting their job
★   the boss might take you up with the promotion
★   you gain another friend in high places
★   if the boss fails in the new job then it is obvious who made him or her a success

So, when considering the job, questions to ask could include some of the following:

- ★ How long has the boss been in the job?
- ★ What is his/her standing in the organization?
- ★ Is he/she well respected?
- ★ Is he/she in line for promotion in the near to medium future?
- ★ How well connected is my boss within the organization?
- ★ How does my boss see his/her career developing?
- ★ Is my boss still achieving in the job?
- ★ Has my boss reached his/her peak in career terms?

If you want to be a rising star then work with the brightest star you can. If your boss is not going places, chances are you won't either.

10. Seeing is believing

Many would be forgiven for thinking that if they work hard then they will be rewarded. Well, this is true to a certain extent – of course it does take hard work to succeed but it also has to be seen and appreciated by those who count. You could be the hardest working person in the organization but if those who should know about it don't, then you won't get the recognition. You need to achieve profile for what you are doing to secure the perfect career.

Before taking on a task, project or job, just ask yourself how much profile is it going to give you with those who hold the keys to your future, and if the answer is 'Not much' then think twice before moving or undertaking the project.

At one time I used to do a lot of work with middle management at Goodyear Tyre and Rubber Company which had an excellent reputation for promotion from within. Many of the managers gained their first step on the ladder of their careers either by putting themselves forward as a shop steward or as a safety representative. These positions gave them profile, as individuals they were seen by the people that counted – those who could promote them. It is a concept politicians use much of the time. There are many social issues which deserve attention but some enjoy far more media appeal than others and you can guess which ones will have more attention.

Who are the people who are known in your organization and how do they manage to get promotion – in both senses of the word?!

'Ability without visibility is a disability.'
Max A Eggert

11. Take charge 1

You are responsible for yourself and your career; no one else is. Employers want you primarily for your current skills and the expertise you have to date; it is essentially a commercial relationship with certainly no obligation to provide you with total job security or developmental experience, let alone a career.

So take charge of yourself. Do not wait for an appraisal or a formal management development opportunity to be offered to you. Get on with your own career development. If you happen to work for an organization with an effective management development scheme based on appraisal, that is a bonus, but don't count on it. Most perfect careers are based on the 'Do it Yourself' philosophy. It is the difference between being reactive and proactive.

'Destiny is not a matter of chance, it is a matter of choice.'
William Jennings Bryan

12. Take charge 2

'Seek and you will find. Ask and it will be given to you.'
    Jesus Christ

It is a mistake to wait to be told what the limits of your authority are. In organizations the more authority you have, the more power you have and the more you can create an environment and the jobs for the perfect career.

When playing rugby a fellow team member of mine would deliberately break every rule in the book in the first ten minutes of the game. The reason was simple – he then knew how the referee worked and what was possible and what was not. A simple strategy which gave our team a distinct advantage.

When you gain a new position push the boundaries of your power as soon as you can to ensure that you then know how to play the management game right from the start.

13. Failure goes with trying but so does success

'To avoid criticism, do nothing, say nothing, be nothing.'
    Elbert Hubbard

Success is about taking risks and taking risks means that you are not going to win every time. But if you don't try you are definitely not going to be successful.

Realism is important in all that you attempt. No matter how well prepared you are, or how hard you work you will

★ not always get the job you want or the promotion you deserve
★ be beaten by others better than you
★ be in the wrong place at the right time and vice versa

- ★ be adversely affected by market and technology changes beyond your control
- ★ still perform badly occasionally and have off days
- ★ not achieve continuous success

All these things occur with trying. Failure is not falling down, it is refusing to get up again. It is platitudinous but if you don't buy the ticket you don't get in the game, and if you don't play you won't win. Showing up and giving of your best is the greater part of success. Take every opportunity to be there, to try, to develop and to grow. Most things in life take skill derived from experience and practice. You are not expected to get everything right each time. Obviously you can't be like the person whose appraisal read: 'He only makes mistakes once but he seems to make an awful lot of them,' but the message is clear for careers – if someone gives you an opportunity or you create one for yourself, then 'just do it'.

'People pretend not to like grapes when they are too high for them to reach.'
Marguerite de Navarre

14. Get known for skills sets

One of the rules about promotion is: DON'T BE GOOD AT YOUR JOB, BE GOOD AT THE SKILLS NEEDED FOR YOUR JOB.

Sometimes people who are really good at their job make themselves indispensable and then their manager blocks their promotion. A regional sales manager, for instance, is not likely to want his best sales person to move to a regional sales manager position elsewhere. Not only does he lose his best sales person, but he also has another career competitor. You have to remember that your manager's career depends on your performance, not on how good he is in providing training or bringing on future managers. It is obvious that the reason why some managers do not endorse the promotion of their best performers is simply because it might adversely affect their own performance and thus their own career prospects.

A way out of this difficulty is to build a reputation around skill sets such as – good with people, good at negotiation, technically brilliant, creative, etc. Demonstrate how good your skills are in the job but do not make yourself indispensable. In this way you do not become limited by your job title but continually demonstrate the skill required for your present and next position.

'If you feel you are indispensable, put your head in a bucket of water, withdraw it, and contemplate the size of the hole you have left.'
David Charles Evans

15. Don't stay to enjoy your successes
Most people stay in jobs for too long and never reach their full potential. The Peter Principle is correct – 'People rise to the level of their incompetence' – but there is the Max corollary – 'Most incompetence at work is caused by boredom not through lack of ability.'

In the fast food trade the preferred customers are those who 'get, gobble and go'. They are preferred because they spend their money, consume the product and make room for others to do the same. You should have the same attitude to the job – get, gobble and go. Give the job your very best, learn as much as you can, contribute as much as you can and when both these things are done it is then time to move on. Do not stay to enjoy your success.

Young, successful people in organizations are called 'comers' because they are coming through. No employer today can offer you job security, only experience. You in return give the best you can but when you have done the job to the best of your ability and you are at the peak performance then it is time for you to move on should you choose to. In this way everybody wins. You gain new opportunities and experience, the employer can exercise an active promotion policy and someone else gets a shot at your old job.

If you are at peak performance and you stay to enjoy your success, then being at the top there is only one way to go and that is down. When you go off the boil and no longer have the zeal you once had, it is unlikely that you are going to be high up in the promotion candidature stakes.

We can call this 'career scalloping' (see the figure below) – keep going up the organization or your profession until you decide that where you are is where you want to stay. Use your successes and achievements to promote yourself not to lock yourself in. Do not become a victim of your own success.

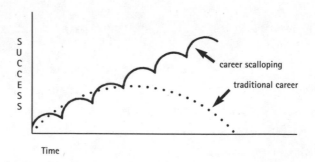

Here are some questions to help you decide whether you should think about moving on:

★ Do you find yourself getting bored at work?
★ Can you solve 90 per cent of the problems quickly with a feeling of 'here we go again'?
★ Do you find yourself with time on your hands?
★ Do you feel that your contribution to the success of the organization is not as great as it used to be?
★ Do you envy other people in their jobs?
★ Do you frequently get the feeling that others must have better jobs than you?
★ Do you get the impression that you are seriously underpaid or that your working conditions are not as good as they should be?
★ Have you been in the job for a longer period than the person who held it before you?

If the answer is 'Yes' to any of these questions, then it is time to think about scalloping upwards.

'To become what we are capable of becoming is the only end in life.'
Robert Louis Stevenson

16. The organizational man
'Either do as your neighbours do or move away.'
Moroccan Proverb

Organizations are not all that different from people in that what they say and what they do are sometimes very different. How often have you heard the chief executive of a family say to the five-year-old and youngest team member, 'Don't do what I do, do as I say'? So the way to discover what is really required of you by organizations or by individuals is by looking at what they do.

Sometimes organizations send strong PR and public messages contained in mission statements, policy statements and even job descriptions but what is actually required from you is something different. A simple way through this, especially when first joining an organization, is to ask yourself a set of basic questions:

★ Who around here is the organization man?
★ Who around here appears to be a rising star?
★ Who is well plugged into the systems and values here?
★ Who is used as a role model?

The easy bit is to ask yourself:

★ What do they do?
★ How do they do their work?
★ How do they behave?
★ What do they give priorities to?
★ What are their values?

Then the hard part is asking yourself:

★ How am I different from them and what do I wish to do about the difference between us?

Hard because either you are going to have to change your behaviour or you are going to have to change your job. If you do not change you will not get on nor, more importantly, will you be happy now you have discovered what is really required of you. If you do not fit your performance will be dulled and your disappointment will show.

'It is easier to move to a new job today than it is tomorrow.'
  Max A Eggert

17. The brigadier and the general

I once was involved with an MOD contract, assisting senior officers in the armed services into civvy street if they retired early. It was one of the most enjoyable and rewarding contracts I ever had, working with such high calibre and competent people.

We worked in groups and in one group I worked with a brigadier. I usually started my counselling sessions with the question 'How did you get to be where you are?' The question broke the ice and helped me to get to know my client quickly. However, the brigadier replied, 'Well, if I had been as lucky as Sir Peter – over there, I would have made general as he did. He saw active service early, got a good staff job, worked for NATO and in Northern Ireland. He was really fortunate in his postings and tours.'

Later, I worked with the general and asked the same question, 'How did you get to where you are?' 'Well,' replied Sir Peter, 'I always wanted to do well and I knew that there was early promotion to be gained in active service so I went to Aden. Then it was imperative for me to get a strategy job so I managed to gain an MOD post. After that I had to have my BTA (Been To America) so I used all my networking skills to get a job in Washington.'

Both were able men in terms of ability, intelligence and interpersonal skills, but the difference between the two was vision and firm goals.

'He who can see three days ahead will be rich, for three thousand years.'
Shigariro Unno

18. Which jobs are for comers?

If you are in a large organization look up the career histories of those at the top. Track back the positions they held. Which divisions did they work in, which functions? Usually there are patterns and themes and specific jobs which are known as slots for up and coming fast track employees (comers). It does not matter whether it is a particular product sales manager position in a pharmaceutical giant, a production job in a car manu-facturer, assistant to the Chairman in retailing, or a particular parish in the Church of England, each post is known to springboard 'comers' to their next stage.

Position yourself as best you can for those jobs. If you can't do that, then plan B should be to get as close to those jobs as you can so that at least you will be in the network of the 'comers' as they move through.

If this stretches your credulity, go and discover what happens to

National sales managers at SKB

Plant managers at Jaguar

Assistants to the Chairman at M&S

Vicars and curates from St Stephen's, Rochester Row

19. Use meetings

Most people sensibly do not have meetings because they take up so much time which could be profitably spent doing the job.

But meetings do provide an ideal opportunity to increase

your profile. Every meeting has an agenda but when you attend you should develop you own covert career agenda which will include such questions as:

How can I use this meeting to:

★ let people know what I'm doing?
★ gain resources for myself?
★ impress people?
★ form allies and allegiances?
★ learn?
★ find out what interpersonal skills I can develop?
★ observe what people want and how they attempt to get it?

When you use meetings as opportunities to promote yourself, your work and/or as learning laboratories you will find that they are always worthwhile and interesting.

20. Be a rodent

Certain rodents enjoy a reputation for acting very sensibly when a ship starts taking in too much water – they leave. Remember that on the *Titanic* even the best officers went down too, so unless your firm gives great separation packages (the corporate equivalent of lifeboats), and fewer and fewer do, leave early. Is this selfish? Yes, it is, but my experience of firms is that when times are hard they become ruthless. Your career needs you not only to be successful but also to grow in a successful environment with a reputation that goes with it.

What sort of statement are you making about your own performance if you are a senior executive in a firm that goes down? Were you not in some way responsible for your own demise?

Here are some signs that sensible rodents watch for:

★ Managers have more time for themselves than they do for their subordinates.

★ Promised equipment is always delayed or postponed indefinitely.

★ Good cost saving ideas requiring an initial investment are not implemented.

★ Top managers come and go quickly.

★ Head count is frozen and shrinks.

★ Important equipment is moved out to other sites.

★ Staff who make long term contributions are not replaced or are transferred, e.g. people from marketing, research, training.

★ Production lines are not run at full speed.

★ Absenteeism is not controlled as well as it used to be.

★ Senior HQ staff and senior visitors are seen more frequently. Smartly dressed people whom you do not recognize are more in evidence.

★ One reorganization is not given time to settle down before another is initiated.

★ Planned maintenance is reduced or run down significantly.

Chapter 2 Working with others

21. Work for your boss

On Brighton Pier along with all the summertime paraphernalia of holiday souvenirs, candy floss and rock, you used to be able to get a brass plaque that said:

> Rule 1: The Boss is always right
> Rule 2: If the Boss is wrong, see Rule 1

and it was strange to discover such a basic career truth hidden away with all the nonsense of holiday tat and bric-a-brac. It is well to remember that the only way to the top is by being promoted and the key to promotion is your boss.

So often in our work we get caught doing things we think we should be doing or because someone in Human Resources wrote it in a job description some time ago.

In Management, things go in phases of popularity; they wax and wane. Sometimes job descriptions and lists of account-abilities have their turn at being popular. The difficulty with job accountabilities is that their value is limited to the time they were written. They are like sets of accounts which give a snapshot of the financial position in any one year. Organizations are not static – they constantly change – and you could easily find yourself working to the wrong or inappropriate set of instructions. Rather like turning up at a railway station with an old timetable – you become out of tune with the rest of the organization and your boss in particular.

Like the popularity of job descriptions, some organizations have mission statements. Now these are very helpful if they are owned by the whole of the organization but frequently they are lifted from somewhere else by the board of directors whilst off on a management junket. Mission statements get delivered like the ten commandments of Sinai but with no explanation or training or commitment, let alone a Moses and Aaron to see they are implemented. Woe betide you if you try and work to mission statements if your boss does not share and work to them as well.

Your boss is the key to your success. If he or she does well then you will do well. Abandon job descriptions, mission statement instructions from the management development department and just ask yourself:

★ What does my boss want me to do?
★ What at work is important to my boss?
★ How can I help my boss most?
★ What does my boss get concerned about?
★ When is my boss pleased about my work or the work of others and why?

And you will find that not only do you save yourself a lot of time but your boss's boss also begins to notice you because everyone wants a good, loyal performer working for them.

22. Network

'I get by with a little help from my friends.'
    The Beatles

Networking is a very popular concept today but it has always existed. There is that popular phrase 'It is not what you know, but who you know that counts.'

It has to be remembered that as humans we have spent more time in tribes fighting and eating one another than we have working in corporations or living in semi-detached houses. Being members of the same tribe is very important in terms of absolute survival and there are still strong vestiges of this instinct today. We have cavemen instincts in twentieth-century corporations.

It is very normal if not natural to do favours for and make exceptions for our friends as opposed to strangers. All things being equal, I will give a friend a job, help, advice, support and information just because they are my friend.

This is not a new thing. In ancient times letters of introduction were given to travellers to new places. Ever since Adam came out of the Garden of Eden we started networking and so did Eve. Mutual support in primitive societies is exceptionally strong. Today networking is sometimes formalized, as in the Freemasons, and sometimes it is woven into a social structure such as the Round Table or more formalized as in the CBI or TUC.

Assisting executives as I do in my work as Career Counsellor, I know that something like 40 per cent of jobs are not gained through employment agencies or job adverts but through networking. As a consultant most of my work does not come from advertising – in fact we don't advertise at all – but from networking. I have to make it my business to know people. People make it their business to know me. At some time we are going to need each other. Achieving the Perfect Career is a two-way street – you help others when and where you can and they at some time in the future may be able to help you. It is not only monkeys that scratch each other.

In the eighties there used to be a sticker in the back of fast motor cars sported by young men in red braces which said 'The person with the most toys wins'. In the tough nineties it should read 'The person with the largest network wins'.

To develop and keep control of your network you should have a set of 5" x 3" postcards and on them keep information on the people you meet in a work or social context who might be able to help you. Besides the usual things like name, address and telephone number, include other things like job, experience, skills, and the occasional personal detail – children, interests, favourite drink, etc.

Networks are like plants, they need cultivating. You can't meet someone at a seminar and then five years later ring them up and expect them to remember you, even less help you with your career. Relationships take time. Keep in touch with cards and update sheets on yourself, clippings of articles you think they will find interesting. Agree to meet for dinner or lunch when you are in their area. Exchange useful information for each other. When a network colleague has a difficulty, think who in your network might be able to help and put them together.

Questions people ask themselves in organizations are different at different levels. When having to do something difficult people on the lowest rung ask themselves 'How am I going to do this?' and at the highest level the question becomes 'Who do I know who has encountered this problem before?' The higher you go, the more important networking becomes.

The jockey that wins is usually the one with the best horse for support – the Perfect Career usually goes to the one with the best network for support.

Start networking – now!

'A faithful friend is the medicine of life.'
Ecclesiasticus 6.16

23. Don't share your long-term ambitions

It is a sad fact of life but it is true – most people want you to be successful but not more successful than they are.

So you would be wise to be cautious and keep your long-term hopes very private. I am not too close to cabinet ministers but none of them goes round saying they want to be Prime Minister. Politicians in America make a real thing about not declaring their nomination for the Presidency. You are not going to get very far – even past the interview – if you express to other aspirants that you wish to be Executive Vice President Western Hemisphere. Bubbles can appear over the heads of recruiters or bosses which say 'over my dead body' or 'get in line'.

All you should do is express a desire to do your present job well and be confident that opportunities will open up for you. If you are quite clear about your career objectives (see section 2) opportunities will occur and you will be in an ideal position to grasp them.

24. Get advice but be selective

'Advice is what we ask for when we already know the answer but wish we didn't.'

Erica Jong

I never mind about giving advice for the proclivity to give it is matched by an equal proclivity to ignore it.

Everyone will give you advice and that is useful but you have to be selective. Professionals in one sphere are not necessarily experts in another but some will have wisdom born of intelligence and experience.

It is said that poor people should take rich people out to lunch for that is the way to learn. Some career advisers suggest that you should appoint your own non-executive board of career advisers – mentors whose views you value and who are further along their career paths than you are. The view higher up the mountain is not only more beautiful, it is usually much more clear and you can see further. Those who are higher up can be of great help in getting your career plans and difficulties into perspective.

Seek out those who have got there before you, have gone where you want to go, and ask them how they did it, what they would have done differently – a polite way of asking what mistakes they made – and if they would mind talking to you once every six months or so. Most executives in the latter part of their careers enjoy and almost have a need to tell others about their achievements and how they were won. It was once said that those that don't take note of history have to relive it. You will make enough mistakes in your career anyway, everyone does, so why not avoid the more obvious ones by getting good quality advice from people who have done it?

'America's best buy for a nickel is a telephone call to the right man.'
   Iika Chase

Chapter 3 Working with self

25. Be personally responsible

'No bird soars too high, if he soars with his own wings.'
  William Blake

Sometimes I get invited to talk at universities or business schools to graduate and mature students and I have great fun asking them who is or who will be responsible for their management training and development. Usually there are a whole lot of responses including the Training Officer, the Graduate Trainer, the Management Development people. Sometimes we get a more enlightened response such as 'my manager'. I then ask questions about the expertise and efficacy of these employees. 'How good are they in looking after your specific needs?' I ask. This brings the same sort of response as 'what do you think of British Rail catering?'.

And then the coup de grâce. 'And you let them be

responsible for your future?' This does not make me popular with the students but it brings home the point very forcefully about personal responsibilitY for one's own training and development. With a little bit of work and forethought you are in the best position to be your own management development manager. Why wait for your company to train you or organize your experience? Why can't you do it for yourself? If you are not interested in your own training, why should anyone else be?

Personal responsibility is a constant theme in this little book which keeps popping up in a number of guises. You have to take charge of your career – if you leave it to your organization, you will find yourself marching to a drum which is not your own.

Self Responsibility means

★ being honest with yourself about your skills and abilities, likes and dislikes, hopes and fears.

★ being disciplined in working on yourself and what you need to do to get where you are going.

★ being realistic about what is and what is not possible to achieve in the short term.

★ being persistent and focused about what you want and not being dissuaded by failure or by the inappropriate comments of others.

★ being proactive in your environment rather than waiting for things to come your way or for luck to deal you in.

★ being self assertive in making choices and taking reasonable risks with people and opportunities and accepting the outcomes of those risks.

Spend money on your own development. How much is up to you but I would suggest not less than you spend on business clothes and dress each year. Strange how we can spend all that money decorating our bodies and yet next to nothing on feeding our minds or developing our skills.

What is to stop you putting yourself on a course or a programme or even organizing a learning set at work with like-minded people. In a self-learning set you select who you want to work with, how long you want to work and what topics you want to work on.

When I illustrate this point with executives or on my management programme I ask people 'How many of you rent a car for business?' and, being executives, most hands go up. Then I ask 'How many of you clean and valet the cars you hire?' and most of the hands stay down. What is the difference? It is about ownership. If you own something you take an interest in it and look after it. Take an interest in your own career and own it.

26. Self reward

A great emphasis in this book is placed on doing things for yourself and the reason for this is obvious – no one else is as committed to your success as you should be. Here is a potential area of difficulty – if no one else is interested in your career you might not try. Motivation theory teaches us that much of what we do is to win esteem, or earn recognition from others or from institutions. Napoleon was supposed to have remarked: 'I have made a great discovery: men will die for stripes of coloured ribbon.' It is not uncommon for us to work harder for others than we would for ourselves.

If you are going to work for your own career then some thought has to be given as to how you are going to reward yourself, especially for the 101 small, tedious things that need to be done along the way. Big outcomes, like achieving the new job, the promotion or the qualification will bring their own obvious reward and recognition but what about all the little steps along the way?

When I work with job searchers we decide firstly on how each major section of this process will be recognized and rewarded. Usually the following are the major steps in the process:

★ The Self Review
★ The CV
★ The First Interview
★ The First 100 Polite Turn Downs
★ The First Offer
★ Accepting the new job

All of these are major elements of the job search process and need to be recognized and rewarded in a significant individual and meaningful way.

Psychologists tell us:

★ What gets asked for gets done
★ What gets measured gets done better
★ What gets rewarded gets done best of all

So for your career the implications are obvious -

★ Set yourself targets
★ Make them quantifiable and time bound
★ Reward yourself for their achievement

These rewards need not be big. I know someone who treats himself to salt and vinegar crisps and chocolate bars when he achieves a small goal; a film for something more significant; a silk tie for a minor success, and an expensive suit or a foreign trip for a major life goal.

'If I had served my God as I have served my king, I would not be going to the place I am going now.'
Cardinal Wolsey on his death bed

27. Stick with your strong points
'Everyone has talent. What is rare is the courage to follow the talent to the dark places where it leads.'
Erica Jong

You don't have to be perfect to have a Perfect Career, in fact it is impossible. No one is perfect, no one is good at everything. At school we are trained to work hard and improve where we are weak. We have to do things again and again until we get them right but in careers a different approach is required. It is not, however, always easy to change the habits one learnt at school.

The advice is do not worry too much about your weaknesses but always play to your strengths. Whenever you can, make sure you have a subordinate or a colleague who is good at those things you are not so hot on. You don't have a dog and bark yourself so if you are weak on details get someone who is strong on the small things. If you are more of a private person team up with a front man who enjoys doing all that high profile stuff. If you are a strategist, get a tactics person, and vice versa.

The higher up the management tree, the easier it is to build round you the elements of the perfect team for you. This means that you can always play to your strengths and look as if you are perfect.

Ned Seagoon: 'Yes, but who are you?'
Eccles: 'Oh, the hard ones first, eh!'
    The Goons

28. Interpersonal skills

One of the many things that is interesting about organizations is that the criteria for success continually change the higher up the ladder you go. On the lower rungs of the organization the emphasis is upon technical and professional competence – being able to do things well and get things done. If you are good at this then your promotion is almost assured.

On the next level, that of management, technical competence is still important but interpersonal skills begin to take on a greater significance. Once you start being responsible for other people, interpersonal skills including those of persuasion, motivation and negotiation grow in significance. What is important here is the skill and ability to get other people as well as your peers to do things well for you. You can be technically superb as a manager but your success depends on getting the technical best out of your subordinates and winning the support and resources from your bosses and colleagues so that your people can perform well for you.

At this stage in your career you are rather like a player-manager. You get on the pitch regularly and practise your technical skills but you have to get the best out of your team.

At the next stage interpersonal skills are important but on the inside track and coming up fast are strategic skills. Being able to see further than anyone else. Being able to appreciate the implications of various options and decisions. Being able to read the situation before it occurs. You just cannot do this if you are tied down to the technology or you are still on the playing field. The view is more comprehensive from the Director's Box.

People who run large organizations well can run anything well. It does not matter if it is Pepsi Cola or Apple Computers, Amstrad or Tottenham Hotspur. Cabinet Ministers can be Home Secretary one day and Chancellor of the Exchequer the next and then go on to run banks. What is important is not so much the technical skills – there are hundreds of thousands of very technically able people – nor the managerial skills – there are tens of thousands of able managers as well – but the gift of vision and strategy – there are only a few thousand with that.

One of the reasons why people get stuck in organizations on plateaux is because they repeat successful behaviour which they have learnt in earlier jobs. Now normally this is a very sensible strategy for success but not always so in organizations. Managers who work harder at being technically superb rather than being good managers suddenly find themselves sidelined and out of the mainstream of the promotional ladder. Similarly, managers who spend too much time literally just managing without raising their heads to see where they are going and the context of their jobs will find themselves stuck in their careers.

The diagram below illustrates the concept of the relationship between the major skill sets. You will see that they are present and indeed necessary in all the jobs within the organization but the amount varies.

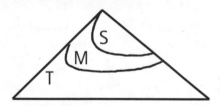

S = Strategic Skills
M = Management Skills
T = Technical Skills

Remember business, like life, is a social activity and you gain more from cooperation than you do from competition and cooperation takes the development of interpersonal skills.

'I never met a man I did not like.'
    Will Rogers

29. Keep up to date

Once upon a time you could gain a qualification and then say 'I'm qualified'. It was as if learning had finished and then work began – two separate processes. This, however, is no longer the case. Technology is moving at such a pace that qualifications get out of date. In times past it was easy to be a bow maker – it was centuries before the gun was invented – but in today's world you are lucky if your technology stays relevant for more than five years.

Even in the soft sciences like psychology, much has changed in ten years – so it is paramount to keep yourself up to date.

It is suggested that an average person reads just one book a year. Just think what you can achieve by reading one book a month in your area of expertise.

The mind is like any other organ – if it is not used, then it will slowly atrophy. Read something regularly and get your mind fit. Jogging for the mind will make you fit for the Perfect Career.

30. Be a star, not a comet

Comets are spectacular when they are around but hopeless to navigate by since they appear so infrequently. Far more reliable are the stars – always predictable, always there.

Organizations need stability to be successful and they need

stable people. It is better to be a star – even a distant one – than put in a spectacular performance on an infrequent basis.

It is much better to be someone who can be relied upon to do something on a regular basis than someone who will do it brilliantly one day but not be there the next. You might achieve fame – more people know about Halley's Comet than about Ursa Minor – but the famous do not get the promotions!! Predictability and consistency in performance are required for the Perfect Career.

'It takes perspiration and not inspiration to succeed.'
Dean Sydney Evans

31. Fantasize

'Imagination is more important than knowledge.'
Albert Einstein

Everything starts with an idea or desire or wish. Even simple desire like feeling hungry or thirsty. The idea comes and then you do something about it to turn the idea into a reality, to convert a dream into an action. Now why should this operate only with the little things in life – why not the important themes? What do you dare to dream for yourself? What do you aspire to? What are you hungry or thirsty for in career terms?

Questions I ask people in my career seminars include:

1 What would you do if you only had 12 months to live before you were struck down by lightning (and you had visited all the places you ever wanted to and prepared your family for your early demise)?
2 How would you spend the rest of your life, guaranteed at least 20 years of good health, if you inherited £10 million?

3 What one thing would you do if you knew you could not fail?
4 Who would you like to be if you could be anyone in the world (living or dead, male or female, fictional or real)?
5 If you could be any living thing (animal or vegetable, bird or banana, fish or fig tree) what would you be and why?

These are not easy questions to answer if you treat them seriously. They draw your values and aspirations from you and your hopes and your fears, your needs and your wants.

Where do your answers come from? What do they mean? Why have you suggested these things to yourself?

Then come the action questions:

★ What are you going to do today to achieve them?
★ How can you position yourself to achieve them?
★ What resources, qualifications and/or network do you need to achieve them?
★ What is stopping you and what are you going to do about it – today?

These questions give you an indication of where the main thrusts in your life should be. Where your heart rather than your head tells you that you should be going. If you're not happy with the direction of your career so far then now is the time to take stock and realize your direction before it is too late.

Wordsworth said that the child is the parent of the adult. In other words, childhood experiences make you the sort of person you are. Career choice does the same. When you leave school there are lots of options open to you but by making choices you later have to live with the implications of those choices.

There is a lovely quote by Quentin Crisp which goes something like this:

> *'It is no good looking after the pigs for 30 years and then deciding to be a ballet dancer, because by then pigs will be your style.'*

In other words the earlier you make career decisions in line with your innermost values and desires, the more complete you will be, the more perfect your career.

Now it might not be completely possible to realize your fantasy, but you almost certainly can get close to it. I once had a young city lawyer referred to me because, although he was well qualified and very bright, he was a total disaster at work. Once we had begun working together the reasons were obvious. Talking through the magic questions it became clear that he was a frustrated rock star, his whole life was rock music. Now, at the age of 27 it was a bit late to become a rock star but all was not lost. He now works for the legal department of a major record company specializing in copyright issues. It is usually possible to achieve a fantasy or get pretty close to it but you first have to do some work on yourself.

This exercise is repeated more fully in the section devoted to activities and can be found on page 423.

32. Advice to the redundant

People who are specialists in this area now tell us that on average everyone starting a career in the nineties can expect redundancy to occur at least twice to them during their working life.

By far the most important point to remember is that it is jobs that become redundant not people. No one can be redundant as a person because everyone can make a contribution and has something of value to give. But faced with redundancy most feel a terrific blow to their ego and self-esteem. It is not uncommon for the individual to feel that he or she has in some way been personally responsible for what has happened. Rather like a road accident where the innocent party says to themselves 'if only I'd not taken that route, or left at that time'. So the person whose job is redundant is similarly self recriminatory – 'Why did I take that job?'

There is also a tendency to self rubbish – 'if I can do it, who would want it?'

If you are sick, you go to a doctor. If you have problems with your teeth, you go to a dentist. If your job has been made redundant, go to a career counsellor or pay for some good outplacement support.

Strange isn't it? You spend years at school and the business of getting a job and managing a career is never really addressed. At this time you need support.

There is very little that a career counsellor can tell you that you can't discover for yourself – eventually. After your 200th CV has failed or your twentieth interview, with that amount of experience you should be getting it right – but it is much better to get it right the first time.

Also, you cannot afford to move into another job that is not right for you so you do need good advice. What is difficult is that doctors' and dentists' services can usually be obtained 'free'. Most people don't think to pay the equivalent of the National Insurance contribution on ensuring they have a healthy career.

Getting a job is a process of being turned down and that is the last thing most people want after they are told by their employer that their services are no longer required. You need support during this period. If you cannot get professional help then join or form a self help group. You will find that you will get far more, and learn far more, from your situation if you work it through with others.

'Security is the mother of danger and the grandmother of destruction.'
Thomas Fuller

33. Just do it

'Many are called but few get up.'
Oliver Herford

Organizations throughout the world spend thousands of pounds or the equivalent every year getting their managers trained in Time Management. The reason for this is simple – the better you are at this essential skill, then the more productive you are. If organizations are prepared to do this with their money, and organizations are usually more careful about their spending than individuals, it seems highly probable that Time Management in one's personal career is going to be of great benefit.

Time Management covers a host of things but there are at least three principles which are essential and directly relevant to the Perfect Career: overcoming procrastination, getting started and goal setting. The last point is so important we give it a whole section on its own (see page 356).

Everyone procrastinates, especially over the large personal projects like getting a further qualification, getting serious about one's network, writing an article, because they are always things which can be done tomorrow, swept to the side by the trivia of today's chores which cocoon us in the familiar and the less challenging.

After goal and target setting, the important thing is just to get started – JUST DO IT.

Just do something for yourself and your career – now, today. Take your career goals and targets and break them down into discrete and identifiable actions that need to be done and allocate a time to them as to when they need to be achieved. Then JUST DO IT. Do something for yourself – now. It is important to remember that you are the only one who is going to take action on your behalf. You are the only person who is interested in your progress so JUST DO IT – NOW – TODAY.

'A habit cannot be tossed out of the window; it must be coaxed down the stairs a step at a time.'
Mark Twain

Here are some Time Management tips and strategies to help you overcome your career procrastination:

★ The worst, the first: do the things you dislike the most first then the rest is easy.
★ Do it for 15 minutes: give yourself just a quarter of an hour every day to achieve your perfect career.
★ Finish what you have started: this is simple and obvious, just finish whatever you start in discrete chunks.
★ Do it for 21 days: make a habit of spending time on yourself on a regular basis each day for a period of 21 days. It is said that something has to be done each day for 21 days before it becomes firmly established as a habit.

By far the most important aspect of your career is JUST DO IT for yourself.

'When a fantasy turns you on, you're obliged to God and nature to start doing it – right away.'
Stewart Brand

34. Self contracting

Because the relationship between employer and employee is so important it is a legal requirement for there to be a contract of employment which covers such things as job title, hours of work, pay and conditions. What some people find helpful in the area of personal career management is to contract with themselves about what they have to do.

Contracting is helpful because it formalizes a relationship and helps make clear what is required from those who are involved.

On my Career Management Seminars all participants have to contract with themselves about their commitment and behaviour, both on and after the programme. Career work is far too important to have people in the programme who are on it just because it is a softer option than being at work. Making a formal promise to oneself about one's personal behaviour is helpful in showing that one is serious about this special enterprise.

Here is a possible personal contract but you might like to just use it as a guide and develop something for yourself.

Draft career contract:

I recognize and welcome the fact that I am personally responsible for my own career and the way I conduct myself at work. I understand that personal success lies in doing the best I can with the abilities, skills and experience that I have. I also recognize that nothing is guaranteed or certain.

I contract with myself that as from today I will set myself quantifiable, time specific and realistic career goals which I will review seriously no fewer than _____ times per year.

Furthermore, each goal will be broken down into specific tasks and activities and I am resolved to spend no fewer than _____ minutes per day and _____ hours per week/month in the achievement of these activities. To assist and encourage myself in these activities I will reward and encourage myself regularly and fairly.

My career management is a significant life activity for me and I commit myself to undertake it with the seriousness which it deserves, knowing that I am solely responsible for those aspects of my work and career which are within my direct control.

Signed ....

Date ....

One person I know actually got her partner to witness the document so he had a vested interest in her success.

35. Get the highest qualification you can – as soon as you can

'Never fear the want of business – a man who qualifies himself well for his calling never fails of employment'.
Thomas Jefferson

In 1944 a Mr Butler, through his Education Act, made secondary and tertiary education available to all who were able in the UK, irrespective of financial status or class. This means that there are now tens of thousands of graduates qualifying each year. Now you don't need a degree to be successful in business – or even to make Prime Minister (in fact, many entrepreneurs, from founders of airlines to retail empires of electronic goods, left school with minimal qualifications) – but it does help, so do GCSEs and 'A' levels and BTECs. Whilst qualifications are not always necessary to be successful in the job because that takes experience, motivation and commitment, qualifications do give you a ticket in the selection race for the job. In these days of significant unemployment employers are demanding qualifications not always required by the job but just to reduce the number of applicants.

Thus the higher the qualification, the better the ticket for the job race for the really top jobs. Do as well as you can with what you've got, especially if you see yourself working for large corporations. Bureaucracies are always impressed by qualifications so if you are able to add some to your quiver, you would be wise to do so. However, do not get seduced into thinking that qualifications help you to do the job or to succeed, as any junior executive with an MBA will tell you – qualifications help you get there but experience and performance in the job count thereafter.

'It takes a good brain to resist an education.'
Max Heinrich Eggert

36. Why do you work?
No, it's not for money – if it were, you would not be reading this book. You want a career and this usually means less remuneration today for more tomorrow or for more personal satisfaction. If it was just for money no one would be in engineering, catering or the NHS.

So if we do not work for money alone, it is helpful and

useful to work out why we work and what motivates us and these are usually one or more of the following:

SECURITY: We want to be safe and in control, for life to have a known predictability and stability. It is not that you do not like variety and flexibility, but that you find ambiguity of circumstances and environments difficult.

AUTONOMY: Here we want to be in control of ourselves, others and jobs. We relish independence and enjoy personal responsibility and are always striving for it.

RECOGNITION: We like the admiration and praise from others for what we do. We discover how good we are and indeed who we are because others tell us. How we stand with others and their view of us, our work and performance is very important to us.

AFFILIATION: This is the need to be with others. Some of us are very social animals.

Once you have realized what motivates you, the other implications become obvious and you would be ill advised to ignore them. It is important that you work in jobs, careers and sectors which will satisfy these motivational needs. A nurse may not be very well rewarded financially for what he or she does, but the satisfaction of knowing you have saved a life must be phenomenal.

A desire for stability would suggest large organizations or the professions would be an ideal environment; autonomy brings about a desire to be entrepreneurial; affiliation points to a team orientation.

37. The four keys for the Perfect Career

To unlock the doors to the Perfect Career you need four very different keys that need to be turned at different times and in different sequences, depending on where you are and what you are doing. You can have three perfect keys and without the fourth you will still find your way to success blocked. You can have all four keys and if you use them in the wrong sequence, you will still find yourself outside in the corridor.

Most people already have one or two of the keys and work hard at turning them in the door and become frustrated when the door remains firmly shut against them.

What are the four keys? They are

★ TECHNICAL SKILLS
★ MANAGEMENT SKILLS
★ STRATEGIC SKILLS
★ INTERPERSONAL SKILLS

With a few moments' thought it becomes obvious why abilities in only one or two areas are not sufficient to carry you through. You could be brilliant technically and be good at management, but unless you knew where you were going, anticipated difficulties, sought opportunities and were able to work well with others, your chances of a Perfect Career would be somewhat reduced.

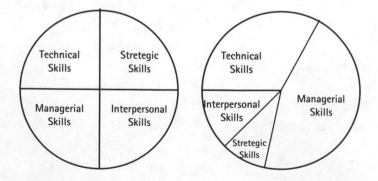

As an exercise you might like to draw your own pie chart reflecting the current status of your skills in each area. Does it looked balanced as in the first figure or does it look more like the second figure, which is the more usual?

TECHNICAL SKILLS: These are the basic skills for the job covering knowledge of how to do what you have to do. They can include producing a set of accounts, closing a sale, designing a project or writing a programme. In other words, fulfilling the duties and functions of the job descriptions. Whether you are working on the bench as a fitter or sitting at the board table on the top floor, you have to be technically competent.

MANAGERIAL SKILLS: These are how to lead, motivate, direct, delegate, supervise, plan, organize, control, administer, monitor and reward your work and that of others. Notice that it includes your own work, self management, so it is important.

STRATEGIC SKILLS: These are to do with vision, knowing where you are going and what is required to get there. This is understanding the context and *raison d'être* of your work, where it is going and your role within that context. With strategic skills you can see the implications of your work and the options that it presents both your organization and yourself.

INTERPERSONAL SKILLS: These are essentially how to get on with others and how to influence them appropriately. This is often an overlooked area and so it has its own section (see page 377).

If and when your career is blocked and the door to your future is closed, review your four management keys to help you decide where you might profitably concentrate your efforts, energy and resources to achieve your Perfect Career.

38. Dress for success

Have you ever thought why it is that different birds have different coloured plumage or why the same species of fish have the same markings? Have you ever thought why the armed services spend so much money on uniforms or why chefs wear tall hats? Why do we put policemen under funny blue cardboard hats, kings and queens under crowns and clergymen behind plastic dog collars and nuns in black and white habits?

Dress patterns facilitate not only recognition patterns but response patterns too. Walk into a hotel late at night wearing your jeans or your business clothes and see the difference in the response you get from hotel staff. They too are dressed differently – the doorman in a top hat, the receptionist in a uniform, the junior manager in pinstripes and the manager in a suit.

Since we only display about 15 per cent of our actual bodies, the way we cover up and adorn the rest makes a statement about who we are and how we wish or expect to be treated. On the beach or at the sauna we all look the same except some of us insist on wearing expensive watches or tattoos to keep the statement going. Why is it that Prince Charles will wear a ring with his family crest on his little finger and Joe Ordinary will wear one with a sovereign in it on his ring finger?

In the armed services these little differences are organized and standardized. All wear khaki or blue but all you have to do is look at the lapels, shoulders and cuffs to see how high up or down the organization the person is. These tell you whether you initiate the salute, being the junior person, or expect to be saluted.

Now business organizations are no different. There are uniforms and dress codes at all levels. It is not written down anywhere but just look at the intense dress cloning that there is. These are the uniforms of life. Now you can decide how you wish to appear. This is very important because if you don't look like a member of the Executive Club you are not likely to be invited to join it. As an experiment, get in the lift at work and travel up and down a few times and just look at what people are wearing. It is not long before you realize that people on the same floor wear the same things and this goes for accessories as well.

'When in the boardroom, dress as the directors do.'
   Max A Eggert

It is nonsense to suggest that you get promoted on the basis of how you are dressed. Your sartorial elegance will not be the key to the boardroom but you try getting there in a Burton's suit!! Not even the directors of Burton's wear Burton's suits. They might wear Marks & Spencer underwear but there are not too many M&S suits, or shirts for that matter, in British boardrooms.

At Sun Microsystems – a very large global computer firm – they have a quaint tradition called 'Dress Down Friday' where everyone, except for sales people, can dress casually at work. The idea is that everyone in the firm can remember the very beginnings and keep up the pioneering spirit of the early days in the company when everyone including the founders dressed in jeans and T-shirts. It is a wonderful tradition but guess what the executives wear on Fridays? Designer jeans, very expensive casual shirts and the best in sports shoes. It would seem that no matter where you are in an organization there is always a dress code. Sometimes it is formal (as it used to be at IBM) and sometimes unwritten (but just as rigorous). It is said that Henry Ford fired an executive because his trousers were too tight.

The implications here are obvious – dress for success. Dress as those who are successful in the positions you aspire to. If your company, be it a Bank or a Burger House, insists that you wear a uniform, wear it well but go to work in the clothes that your boss's boss would wear. Whenever you can, look the part.

'You never get a second chance to make a good first impression.'
Anon.

Chapter 4 Attitude

39. Be positive

Negative people are not promoted. Sales people who rubbish their competitors' product do not achieve sales, employers who malign their bosses or their organizations find themselves candidates for de-selection. Remember, if you run your organization or job down what are you saying to others and yourself about who and what you are?

If you, or the people you choose to associate with, regard work as

- the daily grind
- the rat race
- the funny farm
- the treadmill

it will become just that and your chance of success, however you quantify it, will be minimized.

Positive people appear confident, in control, attractive and they are usually the candidates for organizational recognition and promotion.

It is difficult to be negative and happy at the same time. Yes, of course, there will be difficult and trying times both for yourself and your organization and part of the way through those difficulties will be achieved by being positive.

40. Personal affirmations

One of my favourite quotes is from Henry Ford who said, 'If you think you can or you can't, you're right.'

To a certain extent we are who we tell ourselves we are.

It is all in the head as we are told. We behave in the way we think we should and act according to who we think we are. Like most things this is sometimes helpful and sometimes not so.

We continually have conversations with ourselves inside our heads. Those of you who doubt this are probably thinking 'Do I have conversations with myself?' And it is this inner voice which gives us information about ourselves – who we are and what we are. Sometimes, though, this information is planted there at a very early age by significant adults who are not always correct in their judgement. You will remember that story of the ugly duckling who thought he was just that and presumably acted accordingly until he was told he was a beautiful swan. If you think of yourself, and tell yourself you are just a progress chaser, personnel officer or sales person, it is unlikely that you will make Materials Controller, Human Resources Director or Sales Director.

Junior people act, behave and dress differently from senior people in organizations. If you tell yourself you are a junior person you will think, act, behave, perform and dress accordingly and, mainly because of this, you stay there. If you choose to stay low in the organization, then that is fine but if you wish to move on then affirmations will certainly help.

Now what is interesting about affirmations is that they should be phrased in the present tense as if you are that person already. If you say 'I'm trying to become a Data Processing Manager/Judge/Brigadier,' just think about what you are really saying to yourself. What does your dentist mean when she says 'I'll try not to hurt you'? Also, using the participle or the 'ing' part of the verb means that you're not there yet – rather like that unfortunate British Rail slogan of the eighties, 'We're getting there', to which travellers responded 'Yes, but we want to arrive'. 'I am trying', 'I am becoming' are not helpful statements because you are still in transition, or still on the way to achievement.

It is far better with your affirmations to project yourself into the future – what you want to be expressed in an 'I am a . . .' format. Then repeat your affirmation to yourself on a regular basis.

It is said of one of the present Cabinet ministers that in the 1950s as a young man he wrote on a napkin in a London restaurant '1990 Downing Street'. He has not made it yet – but he is very close.

You might find this difficult to believe, that by telling yourself about yourself you can change your future, in fact change your environment. If you are one of these people then tell yourself, as an experiment, for 21 days that you are a lucky person. Just say it on a regular basis – I am a lucky person. You will be amazed at how lucky you actually become.

There is a cycle of success which flows like this:

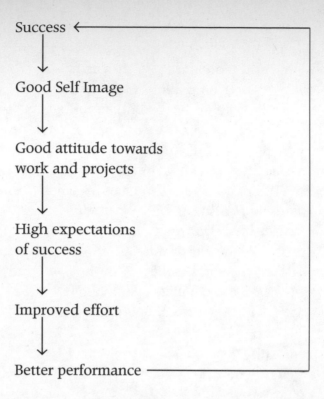

Success ←

↓

Good Self Image

↓

Good attitude towards
work and projects

↓

High expectations
of success

↓

Improved effort

↓

Better performance ──────

and you can see how this is a loop and once you are in it you can 'spiral up' constantly improving yourself, your work and your situation.

Affirm yourself to become yourself and achieve your career ambitions. Remember Henry Ford: 'If you think you can or you can't, you're right.'

Now you cannot expect affirmations to achieve miracles (although some people with an incurable disease have done just that) or reverse history. It would not be helpful for me to say 'I have a full head of hair' or 'I am President of the United States' since I am fairly thin on top and I was not born in the USA. But I could say, if it was what I wanted, 'I am an attractive person' or 'I am a person of influence in politics'. Clearly, an affirmation will not make me a teenager again nor a champion swimmer since both require me to be under 20, but there are lots of things I want to achieve and affirmations will help.

There is an activity for you to do on affirmations at the end of the book (see page 432).

Here are some things to do with your affirmations:

★ Print them on cards and read them morning, noon and last thing at night.

★ Place affirmation cards on mirrors, headboards, desks and other suitable places.

★ Say them out loud; better still, chant or sing them to yourself during private moments.

★ Make a recording of them and play them to yourself regularly.

★ Review how far you have come in the achievement of your affirmation.

41. Develop an internal locus of control

Psychologists tell us that we continually interpret what happens to us whether it is good, bad or indifferent and that there is a correlation between our preferred interpretation and our likely level of success. It is called the 'Locus of Control', that is to say, if I was successful I could take the view that it was because I worked hard at achieving the outcome I desired or I could say I was just lucky. In these two interpretations the locus of control changes from internal – I did something – to external – something happened to me.

Undoubtedly there are some very lucky people in this world for whom the wheel of fortune always turns. If in the case of your career, however, you want luck there is usually a long stand. Take control of your life and your career by developing that internal locus of control, decide to manage things for yourself. When things go wrong, and they will, you can blame the situation, the firm, the government, or you can reflect on the situation and what you can do about the future. I did not get the promotion because I do not have the experience, skills, abilities, style, etc. – these are things you can do something constructive about. Now it might make you feel good to blame your failure, difficulty or upset on something external to yourself but it is not helpful.

Some things are obviously beyond your control, such as a quantum leap in technology making your firm go under or the recession meaning fewer people are buying your firm's products, putting your job at risk. These situations cannot be laid at your door but we are in some way responsible for the majority of the events that occur and next time you can approach the situation differently.

42. Visualize

After fantasy comes visualization. Once you know what you want and where you are going, visualize yourself into that position. Here's how.

1   Find a quiet and comfortable place where you know that you are not going to be disturbed.
2   Visualize yourself into the position – what will you be doing, how will you do it, how will people be responding to you?
    What will your manner and style be, how will you look? What will you achieve, what will be your results?
3   Use all your senses in your visualization – what will you smell, taste, hear and feel as well as see?
4   Practise visualization regularly and not fewer than three

times a week for not less than five minutes a time. (Visualization like anything else takes both practice and time to gain full benefit.)

5 Always make your visualization positive in a situation where you are performing well and at your best.

In sport, top athletes visualize themselves performing at the peak, winning the set, the game or just being first across the line – and it makes all the difference. Remember that top athletes who win, win by very small margins but that is all it takes, just that little bit extra. In developing for yourself the Perfect Career you do not have to be great, just that little bit better than the competition.

'Where there is no vision, the people perish.'
Proverbs 29.18

Chapter 5 The activities

43. The activities

Knowledge is power and the more information you can have about yourself, the more powerful you become. Achieving the Perfect Career is about knowing what you can do and what you can't; knowing what you would like to do and why. The Perfect Career is one that fits you in terms of your abilities, values, skills and aspirations. The happiest people at work I have met enjoy what they do so much that they are surprised they are paid so much for doing it.

These activities are to help you get to know yourself in career terms and so help you when you have significant career choices to make. A useful analogy is that of a funnel. At the beginning of your career you can go anywhere you want. You can decide what field, what sector, what sort of job. Yes, starting out it is going to be on the bottom of the ladder but it is essentially your choice. No one forces you into the Hotel and

Catering trade, Construction, Civil Service, Computing – you choose. So your career funnel is wide and the sides are open as in figure 1.

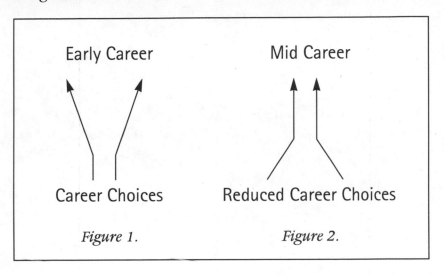

Figure 1.   Figure 2.

But then, because you have made choices they have career implications and will begin to limit you. You become a victim of your earlier choices. Wordsworth said, 'the child is the father of the man', i.e. early experiences affect later ones. In career terms, your 'career funnel' flips and you have less and less choice because of your earlier choices and age (see Figure 2). It is difficult to become a Foreign Exchange dealer if you have been in shipbroking for five years. It is difficult to get into computing if you have been teaching for ten years and vice versa.

This means make your major career choices as early as possible and also keep taking jobs which push the sides of the funnel outwards to give yourself expanding, rather than contracting, career opportunities. Before accepting a promotion or even applying for a new job – however seductive the salary and benefits – consider and review whether the new position will expand or reduce your career prospects in the long term.

Career changes are difficult and expensive both in terms of salary and promotion prospects. Changing is not impossible. However, since it is easier to break a bad habit today than tomorrow, the sooner you make your career moves, the better.

These activities are to help you discover more about yourself. It is unlikely that you will benefit equally from all the exercises for some will be right for you at this time in your career, others not so useful. Some will be more appropriate for younger people beginning their career, others for those who have decided to make a change or who have been forced into job loss or a career change.

'If you arrive before it's over, you still have a chance.'
Max A Eggert

Activity 1
Values at work
What you value personally and what you value at work are important to both understand and match. It is another way of asking the question 'Why do you work?' or 'What are you working for?'

Method

1 From the list below make a card with each value on it (the reverse side of old business cards is ideal for this).
2 Make out five additional cards which say VERY IMPORTANT INDEED, SIGNIFICANT, OK, NOT SIGNIFICANT, NOT IMPORTANT AT ALL, and lay them in a row.

3 Shuffle your cards and then deal out each one under the appropriate classification from Very Important Indeed through to Not Important At All.

4 To ensure a distribution – because some people want everything – you are only allowed eight cards in every column except for the 'OK' column which has the residue.

5 Then rank the most important first, through to least important for columns Very Important Indeed and Significant.

6 Rank the worst first for columns Not Important At All and Not Significant.

The list of values

Aesthetics	involved in the beauty of things
Advancement	being able to get on and do well
Adventure	jobs involving risk and daring
Affiliation	enjoying and finding significant friendships at work
Arbitration	being invited to make decisions and judgements
Altruism	where you can show concern and care for others
Art	involved in art in any of its forms
Authority	the right to direct others because of your organizational status
Benefaction	doing good works for society
Change & Variety	continually changing job content
Challenge	problem solving and troubleshooting in difficult situations and circumstances
Competition	proving your skills and abilities against

	others
Community	where you can become active in local issues
Competence	where you can demonstrate your skills and abilities to a high degree
Creativity	where you can make novel and new contributions through your original ideas and concepts
Calm	working in an unrushed and predictable environment
Control	where you can control your environment
Cordiality	opportunities for you to be warm, friendly and outgoing
Credible	opportunity to spend a lot of time thinking; working on the frontiers of knowledge
Danger	where there is liability or exposure to harm
Daring	where there is a requirement for personal courage in difficult situations
Decisive	opportunity to make decisions about options and opportunities
Detail work	work that requires precision and attention to detail
Excitement	high degree of the unknown in the job where there is novelty and drama
Exhibitionism	opportunity to shine in front of others
Expression	being able to express one's ideas and thoughts in writing or in art
Fast	environment where things are happening quickly
Glamour	requiring personal beauty or charm

	coupled with excitement
Growth	being able to develop personally one's knowledge, experience and skills
Influential	opportunity to change the view of others
Intellectual	recognized as being clever, qualified and a theorist
Independent	being self determined and not dependent on others
Large Organization	more than 500 on the staff
Small Organization	fewer than 100 on the staff
Moral Fulfilment	personal spiritual satisfaction
Physical Challenge	job success requires physical success through bodily strength or speed
Physical Conditions	requiring good conditions for work providing personal comfort
Public Contact	face to face contact with people
Public profile	to be recognized in public
Recognition	to receive positive feedback for good work
Security	to know that your job and your salary are safe
Social hours	contractual hours that leave one free to pursue personal interests
Stability	enjoy work which is mainly predictable and unlikely to change
Status	high standing in the organization that brings respect
Supervision	be in direct control of the work of subordinates
Team work	to work as an acknowledged member of a team
Time Independence	to be able to work to one's own schedule

Travel convenience	easy to get to and from work
Travelling	to travel regularly both at home and abroad
Work alone	to work by yourself rather than be heavily involved in a team
Work under Pressure	work when there is insufficient time yet work has to be completed

Interpretation

Once you have sorted and ranked the cards, look to see if there are any dominant themes in your selection. How many of these are part of or not part of your job?

How many of these themes will be in your chosen jobs of the future?

Are there any surprises in your selection of cards? Are there any clashes or inconsistencies between the first and last columns?

'No man can climb out beyond the limitations of his own character.'

John, Viscount Marley of Blackburn

Activity 2
Career influences

What have been the major 'pushes and pulls' in your career to date? Who and what has helped you or hindered you to get where you are today?

1   Who has influenced you most in your career?
2   What have been the major turning points in your career?

3   What events have had a significant effect on your career so far?

4   What opportunities have you sought or aspired to at work?

5   Why have you left jobs i.e. what has pushed you out from jobs?

6   What has made certain jobs attractive to you – i.e. what has pulled you into jobs?

7   What do you like about your career so far, and why?

8   What have you disliked about your career so far, and why?

9   What risks have you taken to develop your career? What were the pay-offs?

10 How has your job helped or developed others?

'If at first you don't succeed, try hard work.'
William Feather

Activity 3
What did I learn?
Make a list of the major blocks of time in your life and list down what you learned from them in terms of your career and values. Here is an example:

School

> I was good at team events
> I can be popular
> Some people in power abuse it
> Teachers are not always bright or right

1st job

> There are some awful jobs about
> Doing what I am told is difficult etc

Activity 4
Exercise for the future[1]

Most of our limits are self-imposed. To create more options one must change beliefs that limit us. Here is an exercise to help you identify things that have changed for you, and things that can change.

Think of your early life and teenage years and on a separate piece of paper complete both parts of each of the following statements:

> *'I used to believe I couldn't ... but now I believe that ...'*
> *'I used to think I was ... but now I know that I am ...'*
> *'I used to think that I always should ... but now I know that it's OK to ...'*
> *'My greatest fear used to be ... but now I feel ...'*

In the second part of this exercise, think of your life in the future and complete the following on your sheet of paper:

> *'In the future I will not be able to:'*
> *'In the future I will be able to:'*

Looking back at both sets of information, what kind of trend do you see?

> *Are you becoming more or less limited?*
> *How does your future compare with your past?*

[1] Designed by Dudley Lynch

*If you were to rewrite your beliefs to give yourself
more choice, what would your new beliefs be?*

Makes notes for yourself on your sheet of paper.

Activity 5
Magic questions
This is an indirect or fun way of looking at yourself. It is designed to tell you what is important to you and what is not. Some people love this exercise and some hate it. For some it is a very serious way of getting to know themselves, others have used it as a party game at Christmas.

1 What would you do if you had only 12 months to live (and you have visited all the places you would like and have prepared your relatives and friends for your demise and made your peace with your maker)?
2 What would you do if you had £5 million to spend (after you had sorted out your finances, the needs of your family, given some to charity and are in good health)?
3 What would you do if you knew you could not fail?
4 If you could be anyone in the world (Arts, History, Entertainment, Politics, etc) who would you be (you can be male or female, alive or someone from the past, or even someone from literature or film)?
5 If you were an animal, (this includes birds, fish, etc) what would you be and why?

Interpretation

Question 1

The major things of life we sometimes put off because we can always do them some other time. The question here is why can't I do this now; what is preventing me doing what I really want to do?

Questions 2 and 3

Again these tell you what is important to you when all the constraints have been removed. Most of the limitations in life are self limitations and these two questions are a way of confronting them. What jobs or areas should you be working in and at to get close to these areas or functions?

Question 4

Heroes and heroines are very important as role models. This question prompts other questions in this area. Why have you chosen this person? What is it about them that you admire and why? Why do you want to be like them? What is it that they have?

Question 5

This is the same as question 4 but using a different prompt mechanism. In addition, this question gives an indication of how an individual likes to be treated – it says a lot about you if you choose to be a pampered and indulged tabby cat!!

Activity 6
Career anchors
This activity looks at why we work and the satisfaction we gain

from our working lives. Once we recognize our anchors then we can develop our career in that direction. We can also select jobs which will allow us to use our anchors.

Method

Answer the questions that appear under each of the anchors on a scale of 1 to 5 and by working through this it may become apparent which are the more significant anchors for you by adding your scores in each section.

The anchors

1   TECHNICAL COMPETENCE ANCHOR:
    1.1 I like to be known for my skills
    1.2 I enjoy being exceptionally competent in what I do
    1.3 I like being an expert in my field
    1.4 I avoid work outside my skill competence
    1.5 I really enjoy the challenges in my work

2   MANAGERIAL COMPETENCE ANCHOR:
    2.1 I enjoy being in charge of things
    2.2 I enjoy supervising the working of others
    2.3 I like to have things done the way I want them
    2.4 I enjoy making decisions for others
    2.5 I like to have responsibilities for others

3. SECURITY AND STABILITY ANCHOR:
    3.1 I like to stay with one employer for as long as possible

3.2 I do not like to take big risks

3.3 I do not like significant change

3.4 I do not enjoy ambiguous situations

3.5 Security is important to me

4. CREATIVITY:

4.1 I enjoy coming up with new ideas and approaches

4.2 I like being novel and new

4.3 As soon as I can do something I like to move on

4.4 I like my work to be individual

4.5 I like my work to be unique

5. INDEPENDENCE AND AUTONOMY:

5.1 I like to do things my own way

5.2 I find it difficult being directed by others

5.3 I am a better manager than subordinate

5.4 It is important to me to be in control of what I do

Activity 7

Support network

It is often said that it is not what you know but who you know which counts. Managing your own career is difficult when you only have yourself to talk to!! Bearing in mind what has already been said about keeping your long term career aspirations to yourself, it is worthwhile developing a support network. Here are some suggestions.

Someone who knows my industry   _____

Someone who will usually help me   _____

Someone who is honest in their criticism   _____

Someone who knows how to find out things _____

Someone who challenges me _____

Someone who helps me through bad news _____

Someone I can trust _____

Someone who is good at giving
practical advice _____

Activity 8
Career paths

If you plot your growth, development, progress, salary level and overtime, what sort of pattern emerges and what does it tell you? Or, if you do not have the experience yet, what sort of shape do you want your future career to take to be perfect for you?

Here are some examples with the vertical line representing success and achievement and the horizontal axis time.

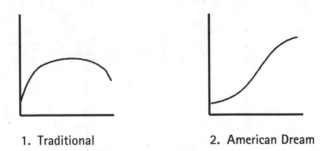

1. Traditional   2. American Dream

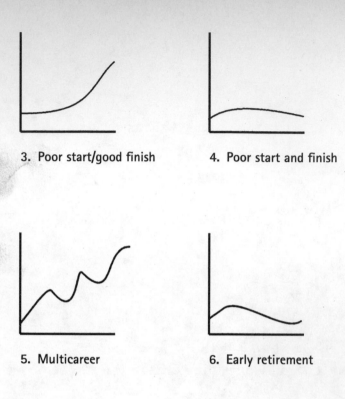

3. Poor start/good finish   4. Poor start and finish

5. Multicareer   6. Early retirement

7. Career restart   8. Drop out

All are possible. What has been the shape of your career to date and what shape do you want it to take in the future?

Activity 9
My career plan

Name: Current job:

Age:

Career direction:

Fallback direction:

Aiming point:

Career development needs to achieve aiming point:

Knowledge/skills/attitudes   Experience

Relevant experience from which to build bridges:

Career plan

Dates	Job type	Knowledge, skills, values gained	Experience gained
(+1 year)			
(+3 years)			
(+6 years)			

Activity 10

Write your own obituary[2]

Imagine that your life is suddenly going to end very soon, but that you have an opportunity to write your own obituary. What would you say? Do not hesitate to be quite frank about your achievements. You may find the following format helpful:

Name ....Age ....
died today from ....
At the time of death his/her principal endeavour was

....

....

His/her principal roles included...

....

He/she always hoped to...

....

He/she made contributions in the areas of ....

....

....

He/she will be remembered by ....
because ....

....

If you would like to develop this exercise, imagine your obituary appearing in a national newspaper. Use a blank sheet of paper to write what you think would be printed about you. Then use another sheet of paper to write what you would like to be said about you.

[2] Based on an exercise by Eric Frank and John Palmer

Activity 11

Personal achievement review

Someone once said 'Those who cannot remember the past are condemned to repeat it'. This exercise is to help you get to know yourself better. It is always a surprise to me to find how little we know of ourselves and what we have done. This activity is a way of reviewing all that you have done.

Method

1   List every achievement you can remember right back to your earliest memory, together with the date. An achievement is something of which you feel proud or something for which you were congratulated by others. It is not necessary to write a huge essay for each achievement, just a few bullet points. Go back as far as you can remember. Not many of us can remember learning to walk but achievements such as learning to ride a bike and learning to swim would be good examples from early life.

2   If you are in a permanent relationship, share your list with your partner as he or she may be able to remind you of things you have forgotten.

3   Wherever possible, quantify your achievements. So, for example, instead of 'made prefect at school' put 'made one of six prefects out of a form of thirty'. Not just 'promoted' but 'promoted within six months'.

4   When you come on to your achievements at work, then not only quantify them but also make a few notes about the benefits of your achievement to the firm or organization and/or other people.

Interpretation

Classify your achievements into themes. What skill tends to predominate? When are you usually successful? What do your achievements tell you that you should be doing in the future?

Activity 12
Construct your affirmation
Think about what you want to be in the future – what sort of job, what sort of skills or experience will you have and so on. Now develop a short paragraph about yourself.

Here are some examples:

> I am a fully qualified accountant.
> I am the best accounts manager in the firm.
> I am the best trainer in the company.

But your affirmations can also be more extensive and more senior, for example:

> I am a self-motivated and achievement-orientated Finance Director with proven international business development skills.
> I am an international management psychologist who enjoys a professional reputation through my work with blue chip firms and my authorship.
> I am an experienced general manager with an outstanding work track record of maximizing start-up opportunities.

Or they can be directed at specific skills or attributes you wish to develop, for example:

I am the most creative person in the department.
I am the best negotiator the firm has.
I write the best reports in the department.

Affirmations can even help you become the sort of person you wish to be.

I am an attractive person whose company is sought by others.
I am a person of value and integrity.
I am honest and hard working.
I am healthy and fit.

In this activity list your affirmations.

Have: One for your eventual job.
One for skill sets you wish to develop.
One for personal characteristics you wish to develop.

Postscript

Some famous affirmations:

'I know that I am an artist'
Ludwig van Beethoven

'I am the greatest'
Muhammad Ah

'I am by temperament a conquistador'
Sigmund Freud

'I am the Resurrection and the Life'
    Jesus Christ

'Captain me am'
    Marisiân Eggert (aged 3 years)

Activity 13
Self-image worksheet
For the next few minutes, think about yourself. You have a self-concept, a sort of mental picture of yourself that you carry in your mind's eye. Think about it and write down a few notes. You might find it helpful to discuss it with a close friend or colleague.

Perhaps the following questions will help you form a clearer picture of yourself.

1 What kind of disposition do you have? Is it different at work? At home? With friends? Describe it.
2 How do others react to your personality/disposition? What does your family think about you? What does your boss think? Your best friend?
3 How does the way you dress, talk, walk, listen, etc, affect others? What type of image do you project in relation to your work? To your social life? To your family?
4   Is the image you project to the world intentional? What self-image would you like? Why?

Activity 14
30 ways to give yourself pro file

1 Write an article for your house magazine.

2 Write an article for your professional journal.

3 Write a book.

4 Become a staff representative or a shop steward.

5 Speak at conferences and seminars.

6 Become an expert in something related to your work.

7 Plan profile opportunities for meetings and achieve them.

8 Take an active interest in the same leisure pursuits as your directors or top executives.

9 Organize social events at work.

10 Arrive at work early or leave later than most.

11 Enthuse about your work, never run down your organization, product, service or manager.

12 Play an active part in your professional association.

13 Talk to one new person at work every day.

14 Form or become part of a users' group.

15 Invite experts in your field out to lunch.

16 Write letters to the press.

17 Attend seminars and conferences and always make a comment or ask a sensible question at the end, stating your name and organization.

18 Give genuine thanks and praise to those you admire and those who help you.

19 Take on a project with high profile and network potential.

20 Organize a learning set.

21 See more people face to face rather than use the internal telephone.

22 Organize a charity event.

23 Take part in a charity event and organize the publicity.

24 Write your boss a brief report regularly once a month on what you have achieved and your objective for the next month.

25 Suggest improvements/cost saving ideas on a regular basis.

26 Play golf or tennis with the Chairman or his daughter, son or favourite niece.

27 Ask a senior manager for advice and guidance.

28 Always dress as expensively as you can in the style appropriate to your organization or profession.

29 Ensure your office provides visitors with the best coffee in the organization served out of the best china.

30 Do as much as you can, but with taste, decorum and restraint, to make your office as executive and as well organized as possible.

'Ability without visibility is a disability.'
Max A Eggert

Activity 15
Personally responsible[3]
On a sheet of paper, write what it is – what few critical outcomes – you need to achieve to be successful.

Next, think for a moment about what is preventing you from achieving them, and list these obstacles.

Now ask yourself, 'If I were 100 per cent responsible for what I want and do, what would I do differently?'

Activity 16
Perfect career questions
1 What do I want to do with the rest of my life?
2 In what situations do I succeed? Why?
3 What are my specific career goals
    For this month?
    For this year?
    For this decade?

[3] After an exercise developed by Michael Higgins

4 What have I learnt today so I can do better tomorrow?
5 What development opportunities are there in this job?
6 How did my boss and his boss get their jobs?
7 Who is the organization man around here and how am I different from that stereotype?
8 How can I give myself profile
    At this meeting?
    During today?
    This month?
    This year?
9 How do people get promoted around here? Why and what for?
10 How can I bend this job
    So I can shine?
    So I can drop my weaknesses and use my strengths?
    So I can develop my skills?
    So I can position myself?
11 Where is the real power in this organization?
12 Who are the power brokers in this organization?
13 What skills do I want to develop
    For this job?
    For my next job?
14 What is the classic career path to get where I want to go
    For this industry?
    For this organization?
15 What is the context of my job? Why does my employer employ me? What is the big picture? What does this mean for my job?
16 What is the market rate for my job?
17 What in my performance makes my boss – happy? – disappointed?
18 How can I make my boss more successful?

19 Who are the blue chip organizations in my chosen field and how can I get into them?

20 What does my boss read professionally and should I read it as well?

21 What do top people in the organization wear?

22 How can I develop a similar interest profile to senior people in my organization?

23 What is the ideal length of time I should spend in this job before moving on?

24 What have I got to do to keep myself professionally up to date
    This week?
    This month?
    This year?

25 If I were to appraise myself, what areas of my performance should I be working on to secure my preferred future?

26 What is the management flavour of the month and what can I do to get up to speed in this topic?

27 What am I doing to keep myself looking good, fit and healthy?

28 Who do I need in my network and what can I do to cultivate colleagues and acquaintances in those areas?

29 What are the success criteria for this job
    For the organization?
    For my boss?
    For myself?

30 How is success measured and quantified in my job
    By me?
    By my boss?
    By the organization?

31 What meetings, clubs or associations will give me maximum profile or networking opportunities for my career

direction?

32 What are going to be the future requirements and skills of this job?

33 What skills are required in my next job and how can I develop them now?

34 What professional memberships should I pursue?

35 Who would be the best possible people to advise me on my career?

36 What am I putting off doing to develop my career? Why?

37 What would be my dream

    Job?

    Organization?

    Boss?

    Team?

38 What sort of salary level do I want

    For this job?

    For the future?

39 When should I get into work and when should I leave?

40 What sort of physical environment should I create for myself at work?

41 When should I next review my progress in this job?

42 When would be a good time to review my personal objectives?

43 How can I reward myself for my hard work and my successes?

44 What career errors have I made and

    What have I learnt from them?

    What has been the gift in them?

45 If I were to be promoted tomorrow who in my team would replace me? How can I develop them?

46 Why am I still doing this job?

47 What is the natural job after this one and do I want it?

48 Who are my major competitors for the next promotion and how can I best position myself?

49 What really motivates me? What are my career anchors?

50 What is my preferred management style and how can I best use it?

51 What is my preferred team role and how can I best use it?

52 What should be the landmarks of my career and by when should I achieve them?

53 How can I be more positive
   About myself?
   About my job?
   About my boss?
   About my product or service?
   About my company?

54 What statement am I making through the way I dress for work?

55 What statement am I making by the way I keep my desk, work station, office, plant, complex?

56 Where have I been successful today and why?

57 What is the best way I can reward myself when I achieve my specific goals and targets?

58 How can I keep my network of colleagues up to date with my activities?

59 What am I doing or reading that might be useful to members of my network?

60 With whom am I having difficulty and what can I do to improve my relationship?

61 Are my goals quantified and measurable?

62 Do my goals have realistic dates by which they should be achieved?

63 Is my CV complete and up to date?

64 What newspaper(s) and journal(s) should I read to best

support my career aspirations?

65 Where have I taken risks and what has been the payoff or benefit?

66 If I were to start again in my career, what would I change and why?

67 What have been my significant mistakes and what have I learnt from them?

68 What is the culture of my organization and how well do I fit into it?

69 What have been the major influences on my career?

70 How can I use my time more effectively?

71 How can I improve my job?

72 Am I doing enough to develop
    My presentation skills?
    My communication skills?
    My persuasion skills?
    My negotiation skills?

'It is better to wear out than to rust out'.
Richard of Cumberland

21 Reasons for investing in this book

1   You will be more satisfied with yourself.
2   You will be able to work at what you enjoy.
3   You will get more out of your work.
4   You will earn more.
5   You will reach a higher level of achievement.
6   You will maximize your potential.
7   You will be able to work to your own goals and objectives.
8   You will be more confident at work.
9   You will get the recognition you deserve.
10 You will be more secure in yourself.
11 You will be a better manager.
12 You will be a better subordinate.
13 You will be in charge of your life.
14 You will be able to create opportunities for yourself.
15 You will be able to overcome difficulties.
16 You will be able to learn from your errors.

17   You will be better organized.
18   You will be more influential.
19   You will have more business contacts.
20   You will be more empowered.
21   You will not have to wait until you are 50 to realize you are in the wrong job and that it's going to be difficult to change careers – or 65 and realize you should have done something when you were 50!

'I suggest that the only books that influence us are those for which we are ready, and which have gone a little further down our particular path than we have got ourselves.'
    E M Forster

Further Assistance

Max Eggert and members of his team are available to speak at conventions, to consult with organizations and work with individuals on career development matters, CV preparation and interview grooming. We also undertake corporate outplacement assignments.

For further information on products, services and programmes, or if you have any questions about this or any of Max's other books, please write to him and his team at any of the following addresses:

UK

Transcareer
9, Hadrian Avenue   and
Chester le Street
Co Durham DH3 3RS
0191-388 9040

Transcareer
94, High Street
Lindfield
Sussex RH16 2HP
0144-4483057

Australia

Transcareer
6/93 Curlewis Street
Bondi Beach NSW 2026
02-9365 5915

or email him on max1@ozonline.com.au